Windy City Christmas

• Quilted Memories of Marshall Field's •
15 Charming Embroidery & Quilt Projects

By Diana Richards
and Jan McGrath

Windy City Christmas

Quilted Memories of Marshall Field's
15 Charming Embroidery & Quilt Projects

By Diana Richards and Jan McGrath

Text copyright 2015 by Diana Richards and Jan McGrath

Publisher: Amy Marson
Creative Director: Gailen Runge
Editor: Donna di Natale
Technical Editor: Christina DeArmond
Cover/Book Designer: Tom Dolphens
Photography: Aaron T. Leimkuehler
Illustration: Logan Wright
Photo Editor: Jo Ann Groves

Published by Kansas City Star Quilts, an imprint of C&T Publishing, Inc., P.O. Box 1456, Lafayette, CA 94549

ISBN: 978-1-61745-322-9

Library of Congress Control Number: 2015948529

Printed in the United States of America

10 9 8 7 6 5 4 3 2 1

TABLE OF CONTENTS

Marshall Field founded the store that bore his name in 1881.
Mr. Field passed away in 1906, one year before the current State Street building was completed.

3

MEET THE AUTHORS

DIANA RICHARDS

In 1999, after her then-teenage daughter suggested that she needed to find her "happy place," Diana Richards took her first quilt class from Jan McGrath. She indeed found her happy place in that quilting class and has never looked back. Diana now designs quilts and teaches quilting in her home studio. She is the Indiana state co-ordinator for the Quilts of Valor Foundation. After more than 35 years, Diana still works as a respiratory therapist. Diana and her husband, Gary, have lived in northwest Indiana their entire lives. They have one daughter, Erin, who resides with her husband, Aaron, in Virginia.

Dedication

To my grandmother, Nina Hobson, who faithfully took me to Marshall Field's every year at Christmas. This has been the inspiration for my designs. She was truly my first BFF.

To my aunt, Mary Hobson, who introduced me to embroidery when I was 7 years old. As a young bride, she was working on embroidered pillowcases as she traveled cross-country to meet her husband's "Indiana family." I fondly remember sitting on my grandmother's porch swing that summer while my aunt patiently taught me the basic stitches.

To my daughter, Erin, who keeps me inspired and amused. She truly launched my quilting passion. I am in awe of the amazingly creative woman she has become.

To my husband, Gary. Many years ago, as I searched for an elegant embroidered Christmas quilt pattern, he suggested that perhaps I should just draw my own. Gary certainly determined his own destiny at that moment. From building a really large light box, to being sent out with lists of threads to purchase, to making an emergency quilt delivery to Chicago, to de-escalating every crisis in between, Gary has played a key role in the development of this book. Thank you for your kind understanding and unwavering support.

To Jan McGrath. Thank you for sharing your knowledge and incredible talents. Thank you also for allowing your creative muse to take this journey with mine. We have definitely followed our dream.

To our editor, Donna di Natale. Thank you for your patience and guidance with this first-time author.

To Doug Weaver and the entire creative team at Kansas City Star Quilts. Thank you for believing in this project and making it happen.

JAN MCGRATH

Jan grew up in a small farming community in Indiana that was miles from most major retail outlets. It's no wonder that a cash register was a favorite toy, as most shopping excursions involved the entire family traveling for the entire day.

Sewing became a creative outlet for a new wardrobe when a family trip was not possible. Just select a pattern and some fabric, and by the next week you could wear a new outfit. Every August the kitchen became the sewing shop for Jan's mother and grandmother as they created outfits for the upcoming school season. The entire family had a skill they could use to create something. Carpentry, electrical, ceramics, oil painting, gardening and canning were all included.

After graduating from high school, the drama of college was overshadowed by the opportunity to take classes in sewing, tailoring, pattern drafting, costuming and upholstery. A marketing degree seemed to round out the picture, and Jan's career in retail was launched. This definite "homebody" soon became the family member who lived in a different city every year. Managing stores, opening

stores, moving stores and finally designing stores for a variety of companies in the craft/fabric industry covered the next 18 years.

The launch of Bits 'n Pieces quilt shop put an end to the moving lifestyle and allowed Jan the chance to launch programs, classes and events for quilters in northwest Indiana. The greatest joy of this adventure has been bringing fun topics to quilters from all over the world and seeing quilters form lasting friendships based on their love of the artistry and each other.

Dedication

To Granny Mae, the only one who believed I could sew at the age of 9. Your love of creating and designing everything has brought me a long way in this world.

To my mother, Gloria, whose pure joy and love of all things Christmas still affects me today. I will never tire of this special season, as it reminds me of you and the magic you brought into our family.

To my sister Marylou, the best cheerleader a sister could have. She believes I can make anything, and I keep trying to live up to that goal.

INTRODUCTION

Growing up in northwest Indiana, near the southern shores of Lake Michigan, was as "Mid-western" a childhood as one might imagine. Springs and summers were filled with adventures in farm fields, riding bicycles and hiking the great sand dunes. Autumn was spent diving into piles of leaves and building "creatures" out of leftover cornstalks and twigs. Winter brought us unending lake-effect snowstorms, dreaded by our parents but savored by all who found joy in the cancellation of classes and the opportunity to construct a snow fort or to ice skate on the creek. Though we were less than an hour from the "Windy City," it was a destination found only on the school bus for an annual field trip to the museum or the zoo ... or that once-a-year magical trip with my grandma.

Each year as Thanksgiving approached, we waited eagerly for Grandma's big announcement — the date of our grand holiday adventure to visit Santa! While that, in and of itself, would thrill most children, it was only a small part of what would most certainly lie ahead. We would dress in our new outfits and ride the South Shore train from Gary into Chicago. Soon the tall buildings became visible and the excitement began to grow. And then, we would spot that famous clock and we knew that our ETA was only seconds away. Marshall Field's!

The first order of business was to view the windows. Each year, from Washington Street up State Street and around the corner to Randolph, a new and fascinating story unfolded, complete with spinning toys and moving dolls—elegant scenes, each more beautiful as we walked.

Next was the visit to Santa, who was assisted by Uncle Mistletoe and Aunt Holly. We had to get our picture taken before we spilled something down the front of us. If Uncle Mistletoe observed good behavior, Aunt Holly would present us with one of her cookies and a special pin would be placed on our collar. After giving our Christmas list to Santa, grandma would take us on a "look only" safari through the biggest toy department in the world, or so it seemed.

Next was the Christmas Shoppe. New and delicate glass ornaments were selected by my grandmother as she gripped our hands, chanting over and over, "Do not touch ANYTHING!" We knew that if we managed to accomplish this nearly impossible feat, a small box of Frango mints could be in our future for that long ride home. One smashed ornament would eliminate that option, so we painfully gripped the pockets of our coats and prayed that we did not hear that tinkle of a shattered ornament.

Having survived that ominous ordeal, the highlight of the outing was just around the bend ... lunch under the Great Tree in the Walnut Room. We would wait for what seemed like an eternity before finally being seated near the 40-foot tree. We so loved searching the tree for Uncle Mistletoe and Aunt Holly, as well as pointing out all the dazzling new decorations.

I continued this traditional holiday trip with my own daughter as she was growing up and believe that she found it as magical as I did. I still have many of those delicate ornaments purchased by Grandma during our trips. They are cherished not only for their beauty but also for the memories solidly encased inside each and every one.

And so, as I set out to design an heirloom quilt to pass on to my daughter, I reached back into my fondest holiday memories and suddenly these pieces began to appear.

Diana Richards

HOLIDAY BANNER

Finished size: 22" x 30"
Appliqué pattern on page 69 and 70

Fabric Requirements

1/2 yard light blue for background
1/2 yard holiday print for border
1/4 yard binding
3/4 yard backing

Appliqués:

1 fat quarter each (print or solid)
    Cream for banner and street sign
    Black holiday print for pole stripes, crossbar and border
    Gold for pole and knob
    Red for pole stripes

Cutting Instructions

Light blue: 1 – 18" x 28" rectangle (will be trimmed down later)
Holiday print: 2 – 3 1/2" x 24 1/2" strips and 2 – 3 1/2" x 22 1/2" strips for the border
Binding: 3 – 2 1/2" x WOF strips

Sewing Instructions

1. Trace, cut and fuse appliqué pieces onto selected fabrics. Fuse according to the manufacturer's instructions. Embroider street names on the cream fabric street signs.

2. Referring to the photo, place and fuse the appliqué pieces onto the light blue background.

3. Machine appliqué using a zigzag or buttonhole stitch.

4. Trim to 16 1/2" x 24 1/2", making sure the design is centered.

5. Attach the 3 1/2" x 24 1/2" borders to the long sides first. Press toward the border.

6. Attach the 3 1/2" x 22 1/2" strips to the top and bottom borders. Press.

7. Layer with batting and backing.

8. Quilt and bind.

This design, as well as the other embroidery designs in this book, makes a nice pillow, as shown in the photo on page 33.

The Great Tree in the Walnut Room was a grand tradition at Field's. The news media carried stories of Uncle Mistletoe combing the forests of Lake Superior to find the perfect tree. The 50-foot tree was brought to Chicago by railcar and then delivered in a grand caravan down State Street on a Saturday afternoon at the start of the Christmas season. As soon as the store closed for the day, the revolving doors on Randolph Street were removed and the giant tree was carried through the first floor to the north light well, where it was hoisted to the seventh floor and erected on top of the fountain basin in the center of the Walnut Room. A crew decorated the tree using a series of swings suspended from pulleys. The Great Chicago Fire left an indelible impression on the city: The entire tree had a series of hoses filled with fire retardant, and a Chicago fireman remained on watch 24/7 until the tree was removed at the New Year. In 1963, a new fire code forced the use of artificial trees in all public buildings.

CHRISTMAS WINDOW QUILT

Finished size: 54" x 60"

Fabric Requirements

1 2/3 yards beige print for embroidery blocks
1 1/2 yards beige for lining of embroidery blocks
1/4 yard gold/cream print for center accent borders
7/8 yard bronze texture for sashing and inner border
2 yards green metallic print for outer border and
        binding
3 1/2 yards for backing
Fat eighths or fat quarters of holiday prints in red,
        gold, light green, dark green, purple, light blue
        and dark blue for the appliqué
1 yard lightweight fusible webbing

Cutting Instructions

Beige print and beige lining:
        1 –20" x WOF strip. From this strip cut 2 – 10"
squares (M and N), 1 –18" x 24" rectangle   (center)
and 2 –8" squares (M and N)
        1 – 8" x WOF strip. From this strip cut 2 – 10"
squares (O and P).
3 – 10" x WOF strips. From 2 of these strips cut 8 –
10" squares (C–D–E–F–G–H–I–J). From the remaining
        strip cut 2 – 10" x 18 1/2" rectangles (K–L).
*Lining is not needed for block K or L

Gold/cream print:
2 – 1 1/2" x WOF strips. From each strip cut 1
        18 1/2" and 1 – 22 1/2" strip.
        You should have 2 of each size.
1 – 2 1/2" x WOF strip. Cut 4 – 2 1/2" squares for
        cornerstones.

Bronze:
10 – 2 1/2" x WOF strips.
        From 2 of these strips cut 8 – 2 1/2" x 8 1/2"
sashing posts.
        From 1 strip cut 2 – 2 1/2" x 18 1/2" strips for
horizontal sashing.
        From 2 strips cut 2 – 2 1/2" x 24 1/2" strips for
vertical sashing.
        Use the remaining five strips for the inner bor-
der.

Green metallic print:
4 – 6 ½" x length of fabric strips for outer border
4 – 2 ½" x length of fabric strips for binding

Backing:
2 – 62" x WOF pieces

Appliqué and Embroidery Instructions

Ornament Panel

1. Trace the ornament shapes from the embroidery designs on page 64 and 65 onto the paper side of the lightweight fusible webbing. You will need 2 small round, 2 large round and 2 pinecone shapes.

2. Cut and fuse the ornaments to the reverse side of the holiday print fabrics according to the manufacturer's instructions.

3. Refer to the embroidery instructions on page 49 for adding the phrase "Give the lady what she wants" to the background fabric.

4. Cut out the ornaments on the traced line, peel off the paper backing, and fuse the appliqué pieces onto the "K" background after the embroidery is traced and stitched.

5. Machine stitch around the appliqué ornaments using a zigzag or buttonhole stitch.

6. Trim panel "K" to 8 1/2" x 18 1/2".

Packages Panel

1. Trace the package appliqués labeled "I" (on pages 67 and 68) onto the paper side of the lightweight fusible webbing.

2. Cut and fuse the package pieces to the reverse side of the holiday prints according to the manufacturer's instructions.

3. Cut out the appliqué pieces. Be sure to leave a 1/4" seam allowance on both the left and right sides. Peel off paper backing and fuse the packages to panel "L".

4. Stitch around the appliqués using a zigzag or buttonhole stitch. Trim panel "L" to 8 1/2" x 18 1/2".

Embroidered Blocks

Embroidery patterns are on pages 50–63.
1. Embroider center tree and blocks according to the instructions on the patterns and referring to the Embroidery Notes on page 49.

2. Trim the embroidered blocks to the following sizes:
8 1/2" x 8 1/2" for blocks A–B–C–D–E–F–G–H–I–J
6 1/2" x 6 1/2" for block M–N–O–P

Sewing Instructions

1. Following the photograph, sew blocks A, K, F and two 2 1/2" x 8" sashing posts to make Row 1. Press all seams toward the sashing strips.

2. Sew 2 - 2 1/2" x 8 1/2" posts, 2 - 2 1/2" corner-stones and 1 - 2 1/2" x 18 1/2" sashing strip together to make Row 2 (sashing row).

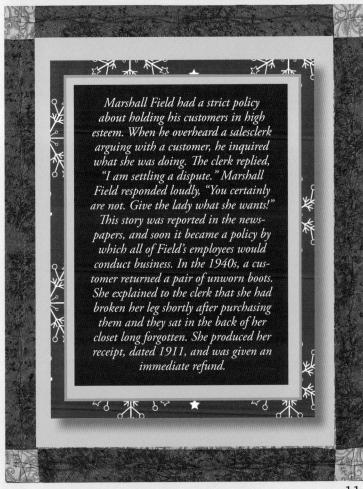

Marshall Field had a strict policy about holding his customers in high esteem. When he overheard a salesclerk arguing with a customer, he inquired what she was doing. The clerk replied, "I am settling a dispute." Marshall Field responded loudly, "You certainly are not. Give the lady what she wants!" This story was reported in the newspapers, and soon it became a policy by which all of Field's employees would conduct business. In the 1940s, a customer returned a pair of unworn boots. She explained to the clerk that she had broken her leg shortly after purchasing them and they sat in the back of her closet long forgotten. She produced her receipt, dated 1911, and was given an immediate refund.

3. Sew blocks B, C and D into a vertical row. Do the same for G, H and I.

4. Sew a gold accent border to all four sides of the center block. The center block should now measure 18 1/2" x 24 1/2".

5. Attach the B-C-D vertical unit to the left side of the center block, and the G-H-I vertical unit to the right side of the center to complete Row 3.

6. Row 4: same as Row 2 (sashing row).

7. Row 5: sew blocks E, L, J and 2 - 2 1/2" x 8 1/2" posts together to make a horizontal row.

8. Join rows 1 through 5 to make the quilt center.

9. Attach inner border strips to the top and bottom of the quilt center. Press toward the inner border. Repeat for the side inner borders.

10. Measure the width and length of the quilt top. It should measure 42 ½" x 48 ½". Cut 2 green metallic outer border strips the same measurement as the width and 2 pieces the same measurement as the length. Referring to the photograph, sew blocks M, N, O, P to the ends of the side borders. Watch the placement of the blocks. They need to finish upright. Press seams toward the outer border.

11. Sew the top and bottom outer borders to quilt. Press seams toward the outer border. Sew the side borders with corner blocks to finish the quilt.

12. Layer with batting and backing; quilt as desired. Bind.

TOP TO BOTTOM TREE SKIRT

Finished size: 48″ diameter

Fabric Requirements
2 yards of beige/cream tonal for tree skirt top
1 yard red for ruffle #1 and binding trim
1 yard gold for ruffle #2
Fat eighths of holiday prints in reds, greens, blacks and golds
      for finial appliqués
1 yard of fusible webbing (recommend HeatnBond Lite)
Heavy thread for pulling ruffle
Backing: 3 yards
Cotton blend batting 54″ x 54″

Cutting Instructions
Beige/cream tonal:
8 units of template A on pages 71 and 72 for tree skirt

Red:
7 – 3 1/2″ x WOF strips for ruffle #1
1 – 2 1/2″ x WOF strip; cut into 2 – 2 1/2″ x 22″ pieces for
      binding the tree skirt opening
1 – 2 1/2″ x 20″ bias strip for binding on circular center
      opening

Gold:
7 – 4 1/2″ x WOF strips for ruffle #2

Backing:
2 – 54″ x WOF pieces

Appliqués
Appliqué templates are on pages 87–94
1. Trace finial sections onto the paper side of the fusible webbing. You will need 8 top, 8 middle and 8 bottom sections. Mix and match as desired.

2. Window the webbing centers on larger pieces by cutting away the center, leaving a 1/2″ wide circle. Following the manufacturer's instructions, fuse the webbing to the wrong side of your fabrics.

3. Cut out the appliqués on the drawn line.

4. Lay finial pieces onto each tree skirt section about 2" from the bottom edge and centered from side to side on each section. Fuse according to the manufacturer's instructions.

5. Select matching or variegated thread to finish the appliqués with your choice of stitch (zigzag, buttonhole, etc.).

Sewing Instructions
Tree Skirt Top
Sew the 8 tree skirt sections together, using a 1/4" seam allowance, to create an open circle. Press seams open.

Backing
1. Sew the two sections of backing fabric together along the selvage edge using a 1" seam allowance.

2. Trim the seam allowance to 3/8" and press open.

Ruffles
1. Sew all 7 strips of ruffle #1 (red) together using diagonal seams. Trim the seams and press them open.

2. Sew all 7 strips of ruffle #2 (gold) together using diagonal seams. Trim the seams and press them open.

3. Lay the red strip on top of the gold strip, with right sides together. Sew the strips together along one long edge. Press the seam open.

4. Fold the strip created in Step 3 in half lengthwise, wrong sides together, matching raw edges. Press along the fold. The gold will extend over to the front of the ruffle to complete the illusion of a double ruffle.

5. Set this aside until quilting is complete.

Quilting Instructions
1. Layer the tree skirt top, batting and backing and baste together for quilting. (We recommend 505 Spray and Fix temporary quilt basting spray.)

2. Mark a 2" diagonal grid on the quilt top. We like to use a Pilot Frixion pen for marking the quilting lines. Use a walking foot if you have one and sew on the marked lines. Be sure to lengthen your stitch for a smooth quilting stitch.

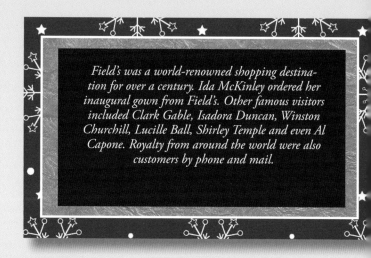

Field's was a world-renowned shopping destination for over a century. Ida McKinley ordered her inaugural gown from Field's. Other famous visitors included Clark Gable, Isadora Duncan, Winston Churchill, Lucille Ball, Shirley Temple and even Al Capone. Royalty from around the world were also customers by phone and mail.

3. Baste 1/4" around outer edge, the back slit and the center circle of the tree skirt top using a walking foot and a long basting stitch.

4. Trim all layers to match tree skirt top.

Attach the Ruffle
1. Divide the strip into four equal quarters and mark with pins.

2. Using a medium open zigzag setting on your machine, stitch over a heavy thread 1/4″ from the raw edges of folded ruffle. The zigzag acts as a casing for the heavy thread used for gathering the ruffle. Be careful not to stitch through the heavy thread.

3. Wrap the heavy thread around a pin at the start and stop points of the ruffle to prevent the thread from pulling free. **See illustration below.**

4. Pull heavy thread to create gathers.

5. Divide tree skirt outer edge into four equal sections and mark with pins.

6. Pin the ruffle to the skirt, matching the marking pins, with the red side of the ruffle facing the right side of the tree skirt. Adjust the gathers as needed to fit the ruffle to the tree skirt top evenly between all the pin markings. Use lots of pins to keep all of the layers together.

7. Sew the ruffle to the skirt using a 3/8″ seam allowance. Overcast or zigzag the seam allowance to prevent raveling.

8. Press the seam toward the skirt. On the right side of the skirt, topstitch a scant 1/4″ from the seam to help hold the ruffle in place.

Finishing Touches

1. Fold the 2 1/2″ x 22″ strip of red in half lengthwise, with wrong sides together, to create binding for the back slit.

2. Sew binding to each side of the tree skirt slit using a 3/8″ seam allowance. Begin at the top of the tree skirt, matching the raw edge of the binding with the raw edge of the opening. When you are about 4″ from the bottom end of the slit, trim the excess binding about 1/4″ from the edge of the tree skirt. Fold the end under 1/4″ and continue sewing the binding to the tree skirt.

3. Fold the binding to the back of tree skirt and stitch in place by hand or machine.

4. Create a 2 1/2″ x 36″ strip of bias binding from the remaining red fabric.

5. Fold under each end of the bias binding 1/4″ and press. Sew the bias binding to the top edge of the skirt, covering the raw edges of the side binding and leaving a tail at each end for tying the skirt around tree base.

6. Fold binding to back and hand or machine stitch. Edge stitch the ties.

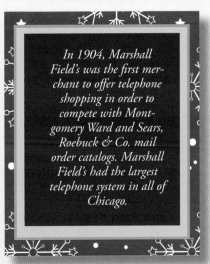

In 1904, Marshall Field's was the first merchant to offer telephone shopping in order to compete with Montgomery Ward and Sears, Roebuck & Co. mail order catalogs. Marshall Field's had the largest telephone system in all of Chicago.

HOLIDAY TOTE BAG

Finished size: 14" x 12 1/2" x 4 1/2"

When a group of ladies complained about carrying their purchases home on the trolley, Field's began a delivery service. People also left messages for friends at the Field's Personal Service desk, so a Guest Service book was created. These books contained an amazing collection of important autographs of the times.

Fabric Requirements
5/8 yard beige tonal for outer bag
5/8 yard beige for inner bag
3/8 yard yard green for bag bottom
    and binding
5/8 yard of cotton batting
8" square of green for tree applique
4" square of gold for star and tree trunk
1/8 yard of lightweight fusible webbing

Cutting Instructions
Beige tonal :
1 - 18" x WOF strip
1 - 2 1/2" x WOF strip for the handles

Beige for inner bag:
1 - 22" x WOF strip

Green:
1 - 4" x WOF strip for bag bottom
2 - 2 1/2" x WOF strips for binding

Batting:
1 - 1" strip for the handles

Sew and Appliqué the Bag
1. Sew the 4" strip of green bag bottom to the 22" strip of beige tonal for outer bag. Press the seam toward the green.

2. Make a quilt sandwich using the inner bag fabric, batting and outer bag fabric. Spray lightly with temporary quilt basting spray to adhere the layers.

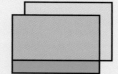

3. Let's do some wacky quilting. Select quilting thread to match the color of the outer bag. Using a walking foot on your machine, adjust the stitch length to be a bit longer than a regular sewing stitch, and simply wiggle your quilt as you stitch. Repeat approximately 3" away until you have done the entire piece. Now do the same in the opposite direction to create the "wacky" grid design. Be sure to quilt the bottom (green) portion, too, to add strength to the bottom

4. Square and trim the quilted piece to 17" x 36" but don't cut away any of the green bottom.

5. Sew the short ends together with a 1/4" seam allowance, keeping the outer bag sides together. Zigzag stitch over the raw edges of the seam edge to keep them from fraying.

6. Rotate the "tube" so that the seam is in the center back. Find the center of the front and mark with a disappearing marker.

7. Trace the tree branches and star templates on page 86 onto the paper side of the fusible webbing.

8. Following the manufacturer's directions, fuse to the wrong side of the appliqué fabrics.

9. Cut out the designs on the traced lines. Remove the paper backing and fuse to the front of the bag, centering the tree and referring to the photograph for placement.

10. Finish the edges of the tree branches, trunk and star with a zigzag stitch. If desired, stitch back and forth across the star from point to point to make the star appear more star-like.

11. Sew the 4″ bottom piece (green) to the top section using a 3/8″ seam allowance. Zigzag stitch over the seam edge to keep it from fraying.

12. To box pleat the bottom corners, turn the bag wrong side out. Fold the bag so that the bottom corners become pointed tips as shown in the illustration. Measure 2″ from the tip and make a mark. Draw a line across the bag at this point and stitch on the line. Repeat on the point at the other end.

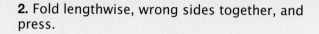

Binding

1. Make the binding by sewing the two 2 1/2″ strips together using a mitered seam. Trim the seam and press open.

2. Fold lengthwise, wrong sides together, and press.

3. Sew to the inside of the top edge of the bag, matching raw edges and using a 3/8″ seam allowance. Press binding away from bag.

4. Bring the folded edge of the binding over to the outside of the bag. Topstitch in place.

Handles

1. Using the 2 1/2″ beige tonal strip, lay a 1″ strip of batting down the center of the reverse side of the fabric. Cut in half to make two handles that are 22″ long.

2. Fold one long edge of each piece toward the center over the batting and press.

3. Fold the opposite long edge in about 1/4″ and then fold again toward the center, covering the raw edge of the first fold. (See diagram.)

4. Stitch down the middle of the handle to secure.

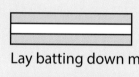

Lay batting down middle of strip

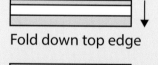

Fold down top edge

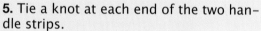

Stitch down the middle to secure

5. Tie a knot at each end of the two handle strips.

6. Attach the handles 4″ in from each side and just below the green bound edge along top of bag. Stitch securely just above each knot.

BAKING FOR SANTA

AUNT HOLLY'S GIRL'S APRON

Fabric Requirements
3/8 yard white print for the lower apron
5/8 yard white for apron lining
1/3 yard red print for upper apron and lower band
7" square white with red print for the collars
1/3 yard green for ties, waist trim, collar trim and appliqué

Cutting Instructions
White print:
1 – 12 1/2" x 18 1/2" rectangle for the apron skirt
1 – 4" x 4 1/2" piece for the pocket
1 – 7 1/2" square for collar

Lining:
1 – 19" square
1 – 4" x 4 1/2" piece for the pocket lining

Red print:
1 – 7 1/2" x 18 1/2" rectangle for the upper apron
1 – 2 1/2" x 18 1/2" strip for lower band on skirt

Green:
1 – 2" x WOF strip. From this strip cut a 18 1/2" strip for
   the flange at the waist. Trim the remainder of the strip
   to 1" wide for the trim at the collar points.
1 – 2 1/2" x WOF strip. Cut into 2 – 2 1/2" x 20" strips for
   the apron ties.
1 – 2 1/2" x WOF strip. Cut into 2 – 2 1/2" x 17 1/2" strips
   for the neck ties. Trim the remaining strip to 4 – 1" x
8" strips for collar borders.

Sewing Instructions
Apron
1. Make the waistband flange by folding the 2" x 18 1/2"
green strip in half lengthwise, right sides together.

2. Lay the white apron skirt rectangle on the red print upper
apron rectangle, right sides facing. Slip the green flange in
between the two, matching all long raw edges. Stitch along
the upper edge, making sure to catch the flange in the seam
between the upper and lower apron sections. Open and
press. Press the flange toward the bottom of the apron.

3. Place the apron pattern on page 86 on top of the apron set

▬▬▬▬	Red print
▭	Green Flange
▤▤▤▤▤▤▤	White and red print

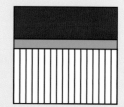

and cut out the armhole arc.

4. Make the neck and waist ties by folding the strips in half lengthwise, right sides together, and sewing a 1/4" seam along the long side and one short end. Angle the ends if desired. Turn right side out. Press.

5. Pin the unfinished edge of the neck ties 1/4" inside of the edge of apron top, one on each side. Lay the tails of the neck ties toward the middle of the apron to avoid catching them in the seams.

6. Pin the unfinished edge of the waist ties at the edge of the green flange on each side of the apron. Lay the tails toward the middle of the apron to avoid catching them in the seams.

Collar

1. Sew the 1" green strips onto the 7" square white with red print to create a border. Press toward green.

2. Place bordered square right side down on solid white 7 1/2" square. Sew around outer edge using a 1/4" seam allowance.

3. Cut white/red square with green trim in half along the diagonal. Turn both sections right side out and press.

4. Lay the collar pieces along the neck edge 1/4" in from each side. Pin.

Finishing the Apron

1. Flip the entire apron right side down on top of the lining fabric.

2. Starting in the middle of the bottom edge, sew around the entire outer edge of the apron, leaving a 3" opening along the bottom for turning. Trim away the excess lining fabric. Clip the curves on the upper apron and turn right side out through the bottom opening. Press.

3. Edge stitch around the entire apron. Be sure to catch the ties at the waist and neck and the opening along the bottom to sew it shut.

4. Make the pocket by sewing the pocket piece to the pocket lining, right sides together, with a 1/4" seam. Leave a small opening along bottom edge for turning. Turn right side out. Press.

5. Trace, cut and fuse the applique design on page 76 to the pocket front. Zigzag stitch around the edges.

6. Topstitch in place along left front side of apron skirt.

7. Add buttons to apron front. Tack down collar points.

At the turn of the century, Yard Goods was one of the most popular departments at Field's. The finest linens, silks, wools and laces were imported from all over the world.

UNCLE MISTLETOE'S BOY'S APRON

Fabric Requirements

5/8 yard red for apron front and lining
1/3 yard green for apron ties, lower band and trim
1 fat quarter white print for the scarf appliqué and pockets

Cutting Instructions

Red:
1 – 16 1/2" square for apron front. Use the remainder for the apron lining.

Green:
1 – 2 1/2" x WOF strip. Cut into 2 – 2 1/2" x 20" strips for the neck ties.
1 – 2 1/2" x WOF strip. Cut into 2 – 2 1/2" x 17" strips for the waist ties.
1 – 2 1/2" x 16 1/2" strip for the lower apron band
4 – 1" x 3 1/2" strips for the top of the mitten pocket trim
1 – 5/8" x 18" strip for trim on scarf

Sewing Instructions

1. Sew the 2 1/2" x 16 1/2" green band to the lower edge of the red 16 1/2" x 16 1/2" strip. Press.

2. Using the pocket pattern on page 77, cut 4 pockets. Be sure to cut 2 and 2 reversed.

3. Sew a 1" green pocket trim to top of all 4 pockets. Press toward the green.

4. Sew 2 pocket pieces together, right sides facing. Sew around the mitten pocket, leaving an opening at the top for turning. Turn right side out and press, pressing the open seam to the inside.

5. Pin the mitten pockets onto apron front as indicated on the pattern. Topstitch in place.

Appliqués

1. Trace the appliqué patterns for the scarf on page 77 onto the paper side of fusible webbing. There are 3 scarf sections and 2 trim pieces.

2. Cut around the appliqué designs and fuse to the reverse side of the white fabric. Cut out scarf pieces on the traced line.

3. Use the photo as a guide to fuse the scarf and trim to the apron front.

4. Stitch around the appliqué using a zigzag or

buttonhole stitch.

Finishing the Apron

1. Place the apron pattern on page 78 on top of the apron set and cut out the armhole arc.

2. Make the neck and waist ties by folding the strips in half lengthwise, right sides together, and sewing a 1/4″ seam along the long side and one short end. Angle the ends if desired. Turn right side out. Press.

3. Lay the entire apron front, right side down, onto the remaining red fabric lining.

4. Stitch around the apron using a 1/4″ seam. Leave a small opening at bottom for turning. Clip the armhole curves. Turn right side out and press, pressing the open seam to the inside.

5. Edge stitch around the entire apron. Be sure to catch the ties at the waist and neck and the open-ing along the bottom to sew it shut.

6. Stitch a decorative line down center of apron from scarf through lower band to simulate the front edge of the coat.

7. Attach 2 buttons to simulate coat opening.

Field's introduced Uncle Mistletoe in 1946 and Aunt Holly in 1948 as part of the store's Christmas celebration. They became wildly popular - at times, it seemed, even more so than Santa. Eventually they joined Santa in the Cloud Cottage on the eighth floor. A child's well-behaved visit with Santa would be rewarded with a "Kindness Club" button.

The Field Museum of Natural History was founded with $1 million contributed by Marshall Field. He later added a second $1 million, and when he died in 1906, he left $8 million to the museum in his will.

CHILD'S TOQUE (CHEF'S HAT)

Fabric Requirements

Measure the diameter of the child's head to check fit of toque. If larger than 19″, more fabric may be needed.
1/8 yard for hatbands: black for boy's toque, red for girl's toque
3/4 yard white with red print for hatband and gathered top of toque
6″ x WOF strip for hat band lining
3″ x 3″ green for appliqué

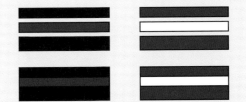

Cutting Instructions

Circle diameter equals the hatband size.

Black or red:
1 – 2 1/2″ x 20″ strip for the lower section of the hatband
1 – 2 1/4″ x 20″ strip for the upper section of the hatband

White with red print:
1 – 2″ x 20″ strip for middle of hatband
1 – 20″ circle for top of toque
1 – 6″ x 20″ strip for hat band lining

Sewing Instructions

1. Sew a strip set using the black/red 2 1/4″ x 20″ strip, the 2″ x 20″ white with red print strip and the 2 1/2″ x 20″ black/red strip. Press seams away from the middle strip.

2. Lay the strip set on the 6″ x 20″ hatband lining, right sides facing. Sew long edges with 1/4″ seam allowance. Turn through the end. Press.

3. Sew the short ends together, right sides facing, to form a continuous loop. Press and turn right side out.

4. Sew a long gathering stitch along the outer edge of the 20″ circle.

5. Divide circle into four equal pieces by folding in half and half again. Place a pin on each fold. Do the same on the hatband.

6. Sew top edge of band to the circle, matching pins and adjusting the gathers as you sew.

7. Zigzag the raw edge of this seam with a wide stitch to prevent fraying.

HOLIDAY LANE

GRAND TREE WALL HANGING

Finished size: 28" x 32"

Fabric Requirements
3/4 yard beige print for center block and pieced border
5/8 yard beige fabric for center block lining
1 yard copper/bronze accent fabric for pieced
    and outer borders
1 yard for backing
1/4 yard for binding

Cutting Instructions

Beige print:
1 – 18" x 24" rectangle for the center embroidered block
2 – 2 1/2" x WOF strips. Cut into 18 – 2 1/2" x 4 1/2"
    rectangles for the pieced border

Beige:
1 – 18" x 24" rectangle to use as backing for the
    embroidered block

Copper/bronze accent fabric:
3 – 2 1/2" x WOF strips. Cut into 40 – 2 1/2" squares for
    the pieced border. Reserve 4 to use as
    cornerstones.
4 – 4 1/2" x WOF strips. Recut into 2 – 4 1/2" x 24 1/2" and 2 – 4 1/2" x 28 1/2" strips
    for the outer border.
3 – 2 1/2" x WOF strips for the binding

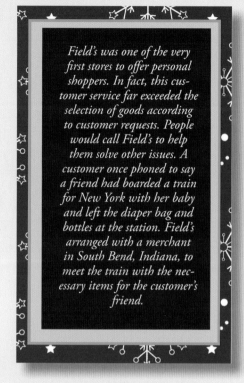

Field's was one of the very first stores to offer personal shoppers. In fact, this customer service far exceeded the selection of goods according to customer requests. People would call Field's to help them solve other issues. A customer once phoned to say a friend had boarded a train for New York with her baby and left the diaper bag and bottles at the station. Field's arranged with a merchant in South Bend, Indiana, to meet the train with the necessary items for the customer's friend.

Embroidery Instructions
Refer to embroidery instructions on page 49 and the Christmas Windows Quilt on page 11 to embroider the tree.

Trim embroidered block to 16 1/2" x 20 1/2".

Sewing Instructions
1. Draw a diagonal line on the wrong side of 36 of the 2 1/2" accent fabric squares.

2. Place a 2 1/2" accent square on the left side of a beige 2 1/2" x 4 1/2" rectangle. Sew on the
drawn line. Press the corner back, checking alignment with corner below. They must match.
Cut away the excess fabric, leaving a 1/4" seam allowance. Make 18 units.

3. Using the remaining 18 – 2 1/2" squares, repeat Step 2 but place the 2 1/2" accent square on the right side. Be sure to check the angle of the drawn line.

4. Sew 4 units end-to-end to make a row. Sew a 2 1/2" square (reserved for the cornerstone) to each end to create the top and bottom borders. Make 2. Press seam allowances open.

5. Sew 5 units end-to-end to make the side borders. Make 2. Press seam allowances open.

6. Sew the pieced borders to the embroidered center block. Attach the side borders first, then the top and bottom borders.

7. Sew the 24 1/2" outer border strips to the sides. Press the seams toward the outer border.

8. Add the 28 1/2" border strips to the top and bottom. Press seams toward the outer border.

9. Layer, quilt and bind.

Terry Nelson, Jan's pattern tester and embroidery queen, did the beautiful embroidery on the Grand Tree Wall Hanging. Thank you so much, Terry.

The first of the Marshall Field's clocks was installed at the corner of Washington and State streets on November 26, 1897. Another was installed later at the corner of State and Randolph. They are each made of more than 7 tons of cast bronze and stand 17.5 feet above the sidewalk. "Under the clock at Field's" is a famous place to meet.

ORNAMENT PILLOW

Finished size: 12" x 22"

Embroidery designs are on pages 64 and 65

Fabric Requirements

1/4 yard tone-on-tone beige print for pillow center
1/4 yard solid beige or muslin for lining the embroidery
2" x WOF strip of red for the flange
3/4 yard green holiday print for the border and backing
Fiberfill for stuffing

Cutting Instructions

Tone-on-tone beige print and solid beige or muslin:
1 - 9" x 18" rectangle from each for the pillow center and lining

Red:
2 - 1" x WOF strips for the folded flange. Cut into 2 pieces 1" x 17 ½" and 2 pieces 1" x 7 ½"

Green holiday print:
3 - 3" x WOF strips for the border
13 1/2" x 22 1/2" rectangle for the backing

Sewing Instructions

1. Trace the designs on pages 64 and 65 onto the center panel.

2. Back the center panel with the lining and embroider the designs. Be sure to stitch through both the center and lining fabrics.

3. Press and trim the center panel to 7 1/2" x 17 1/2", making sure the design is centered.

4. Fold the red 1" flange strips in half, wrong sides together. Press.

5. Cut and baste the flange strips to the top and bottom of the embroidered panel. The fold should face toward the center.

6. Cut and baste the flange strips to the sides of the pillow, overlapping the top and bottom strips.

7. Attach the top and bottom border strips first, being sure to catch the flange in the seam.

8. Attach the side border strips, again being sure to catch the flange. Press.

9. Layer the pillow front and back, right sides together. Stitch with a 1/4" seam allowance. Leave a 4" opening along one end for turning.

10. Turn right side out. Press.

11. Stuff with fiberfill to desired fullness and stitch the opening closed.

HOLIDAY STOCKINGS

Finished size:
Large – 18″ x 24″
Small – 12″ x 18″

Fabric Requirements:

Large Stocking
3/4 yard holiday print
2/3 yard for cuff points, binding and hanger
1 yard fusible quilter's fleece;
cut into a 3/4 yard cut and a 10 1/2″ cut.
1/3 yard lining
Fiberfill

Small Stocking
1/2 yard holiday print
2/3 yard for cuff points, binding and hanger
2/3 yard fusible quilter's fleece
1/4 yard lining
Fiberfill

Frango Mints were a famous treat at Field's sweet treat beginning in 1929. They are still sold today by the Macy's store.

Sewing Instructions

Stocking
1. Trace the templates on pages 80–85 onto freezer paper. Cut out, leaving about 1/2″ all the way around the traced line.

2. Fuse the quilter's fleece to the wrong side of the holiday print and quilt as desired.

3. Fold the quilted fabric in half, right sides together.

4. Lay the stocking template on top of the folded fabric and press. You may also want to pin in a few places.

5. Cut out on the traced line.

6. Remove the template and sew the pieces together using a 1/4″ seam allowance. Leave the top open.

7. Clip the curves and turn the stocking right side out.

8. Starting at the toe, stuff with fiberfill tightly to the heel section. Set aside.

Lining

1. Fold lining fabric in half, right sides together.

2. Press and pin the stocking template onto the lining.

3. Trace around the template, stopping at the heel. Do not trace toe. This allows for the lining to act as a pocket for stocking stuffers.

4. Stitch around the outer edge of the lining with 1/4" seam, leaving the top open. Do not turn.

5. Place lining inside stocking with the wrong side of the lining facing the wrong side of the stocking.

6. Pin the top edges and stitch together with a 1/4" seam.

Cuff Points

1. Cut a 2 1/2" x WOF strip from the cuff fabric. Set this aside for making the binding and hanger.

2. From the remaining cuff fabric, cut 2 – 10 1/2" x WOF strips. (for small stocking, cut 2 – 8" x WOF strips.) Reserve one piece for cuff lining.

3. Fuse quilter's fleece to the wrong side of one of the 10 1/2" strips (8" for strip for small stocking) of cuff fabric.

4. Quilt as desired.

5. Layer quilted fabric piece and reserved lining piece right sides together.

6. Using the point template on page 79, trace and cut 4 points. Leave the fabric layered for easy sewing. Pinning will help keep the layers together.

7. Sew a 1/4" seam down the long sides of the cuff points. Leave the tops open for turning. Stitch all 4 points.

8. Turn the points right side out and press.

9. Working from the outer edge of the stocking, center one point over the front seam and one over the back seam. Center the remaining two points between the front and back. Baste in place with a 1/4" seam allowance.

Binding

1. To make the binding, use the 2 1/2" cuff fabric strip that was set aside. Fold in half lengthwise, wrong sides together, and press.

2. Sew the binding to the inside of the stocking with a 3/8" seam allowance (to allow for bulk). Trim the excess fabric and set aside for the hanging loop. Press toward the binding.

3. Fold over the binding to the stocking front and hand or machine stitch in place.

Hanging Loop

1. Cut a 5" piece from the remainder of the binding strip.

2. Open the strip and fold the raw edges to the inside to meet at the middle. Fold again along the center fold.

3. Stitch along the outer edges. The piece should now measure 1/2" x 5".

4. Fold the loop in half and place it inside the top of the stocking with the raw edges even with stocking top.

5. Attach the loop by stitching on the same line as the binding.

6. Fold the hanging loop up and reinforce by stitching through the loop and the binding, enclosing the raw edges.

THE WALNUT ROOM

Treat Yourself.

In 1890, a millinery clerk named Mrs. Herring offered her lunch of chicken pot pie to two female shoppers. (At that time, unaccompanied women could not be served in restaurants.) The women were so impressed that they arranged to bring in a few friends for lunch several days later. Marshall Field realized the logic of keeping his customers in the store and soon opened the first Tea Room. On the first day, 56 ladies were served lunch; a year later, the restaurant averaged 1,500 meals per day. Today, the Walnut Room serves as many as 5,000 meals per day. Mrs. Herring's Chicken Pot Pie is still a popular entrée on the menu.

TABLE FOR TWO, PLEASE

Fabric Requirements
Placemats: 12" x 18" (makes two)
1/2 yard cream tonal for front
1/2 yard holiday print for back
1 yard green print for binding and tree appliqués
1/2 yard cotton batting
2" x 4" piece of gold for star appliqués
3" square of brown for tree trunk appliqués

Napkins: 16" square (makes two)
1/2 yard each of 2 holiday prints for front and back

Tea Cozy: 9"w x 10"h x 7"d
3/8 yard cream tonal
3/8 yard muslin or other fabric for the lining
1/4 yard green holiday print for binding and tree
    appliqués
2" x 4" gold for star on trees
3" square brown for tree trunk
1/2 yard cotton batting

Server's Apron: 35" long
2 1/2 yards solid white for apron
1/2 yard red print for ribbon appliqué
1/8 yard each of 3 or 4 holiday prints for appliquéd
    ornaments
6" x WOF strip of Décor-Bond heavy fusible interfacing for waistband

Cutting Instructions
Placemats
2 – 13" x 19"rectangles from the cream tonal and
    holiday print
2 – 13" x 19" rectangles of cotton batting
4 – 6 1/2" x WOF strips for wide binding

Napkins
2 – 16 1/2" squares from each of the 2 holiday
prints. Total of 4 squares.

Tea Cozy
1 – 12" x 33" rectangle from both the outer fabric
and the lining. 1 – 1 ½" x 8" strip of cream for the
cozy handle.

Green
2 – 2 1/2" x WOF strips for binding
Use the remainder for tree appliqués.

Batting
1 – 3/4" x 8" strip for handle

Server's Apron White
2 – 6" x WOF strips waist ties.
1 – 6" x 26" strip for waistband
1 – 42" x 70" rectangle for apron skirt

Interfacing
1 – 6" x 26" strip of Décor-Bond for waistband.

Sewing Instructions
Placemats
1. Make a quilt sandwich by layering the placemat top, batting and backing. Quilt using a wacky grid design at 3" spacing. Seepage 18 for quilting instructions.

2. Trim quilted placemats to 12" x 18".

3. Sew the two 6 1/2" binding strips together to make one long strip using a diagonal seam. Fold in half lengthwise, wrong sides together, and press.

4. Attach the binding to the top of the placemat using a 1" seam allowance.

5. Press the binding away from placemat. Fold to the reverse side and hand or machine stitch.

6. Trace the appliqué pattern on page 86 onto the paper side of the fusible webbing.

7. Fuse the webbing to the reverse side of the appropriate green, brown and gold fabrics.

8. Fuse and stitch the appliqué in left corner of each mat.

Napkins
1. Place one of each holiday print together, right sides facing. Sew around all four sides using a 1/4" seam, leaving about a 2" opening on one side for turning.

2. Turn right side out. Press

3. Edge stitch 1/8" from outer edge of the napkin using a reduced stitch length.

Tea Cozy
1. Make a quilt sandwich by layering the cream top, batting and lining fabrics.

2. Quilt using a wacky wave design. See instructions on page 18.

3. Trim to 11 1/2" x 32".

4. Fold the quilted piece in half and sew together along the short end using a 3/8" seam.

5. Bind top and bottom with the green 2 1/2" strips.

6. Measure 9 inches from seam, place a pin to mark spot (front of cozy). Measure 7" from that spot and place another pin to mark spot (side of cozy).

7. Continue with another 9" measurement (back of cozy) and one more 7" (side of cozy). Place pins to mark measurements.

8. Bring pins together to form a pleat. Press to crease folds.

9. Add appliqué trees to front and rear center panels.

10. Make the handle by placing the small strip of batting down the center of the wrong side of the green 1 1/2" x 8" handle strip.

11. Fold the top edge of the fabric toward the center over the batting.

12. Double fold the bottom edge up to cover the batting and the top edge of the fabric.

13. Stitch to secure the layers.

14. Tie a knot in both ends of the handle strap. Sew the handle in the center of the top of the cozy, just below the binding.

Server's Apron

1. Fold the 42" x 70" apron rectangle in half width-wise, right sides together. The folded piece should measure 42" x 35".

2. Sew down both long sides using a 1/4" seam allowance. Leave top open.

Leave top open

Fold

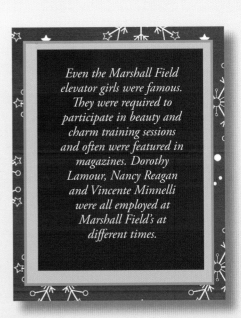

Even the Marshall Field elevator girls were famous. They were required to participate in beauty and charm training sessions and often were featured in magazines. Dorothy Lamour, Nancy Reagan and Vincente Minnelli were all employed at Marshall Field's at different times.

3. Turn right side out and press. You have just hemmed all three sides of the apron!

4. Topstitch all three sides about 1/8″ from the edge.

5. Run 2 rows of gathering stitches along the top opening of the apron, keeping both layers together.

Appliqué

1. Trace the ribbon and ornament appliqué patterns on pages 73–75 onto the paper side of the fusible webbing. Cut out about 1/4″ outside the traced line.

2. Fuse the appliqué pieces to the reverse side of the appropriate appliqué fabrics. Cut out on the traced line.

3. Using the diagram below as a guide, fuse the ribbons and ornaments along the side of the front of the apron.

4. Embroider the gold strings and machine appliqué with a decorative stitch to finish the edges.

Ties

1. Make the waist ties by folding a 6″ x 42″ strip in half lengthwise, right sides together. Sew a 1/4″ seam along the long edge. Make a diagonal point at one end of the strip.

2. Turn right side out and press. Repeat for the second tie.

Attach the Waistband and Ties

1. Fuse the Décor-Bond interfacing to the wrong side of the waistband strip.

2. Fold the waistband in half lengthwise. Press to crease.

3. Fold under a 1/4″ seam allowance on both short ends and along one long side. Press.

4. Pin the unfolded edge of the waistband to the top edge of the back of the apron, right sides together, gathering the apron evenly between the edges of the waistband. Sew with a 1/4″ seam. Press the seam toward the waistband.

5. Fold the waistband to the front of the apron and pin, making sure the folded edge covers the seam line.

6. Tuck the open end of each tie into the short ends of the folded waistband and pin in place. Fold or pleat the tie if needed.

7. Edge stitch along three sides of the waistband, concealing all raw edges and securing the ties and the front edge of the waistband.

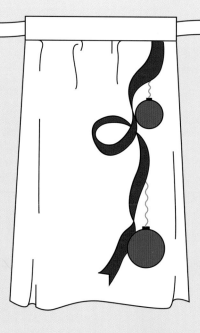

MENSWEAR

PAPPY JACK'S CHRISTMAS TIE QUILT

Finished size: 65" x 74"

The Men's Department was on the second floor of Marshall Field's. Each Christmas, I (Diana) would search for the perfect tie for my dad from among all the wonderful holiday designs. A few years ago, my family physician, Dr. Lauren Harting, brought me about four dozen dress shirts belonging to her late father, Jack. She asked me to design some quilts with them, and I decided that dress shirts must have ties.

The original quilt used an array of Civil War prints for the ties. When we began writing this book, I asked Dr. Harting if I might replicate the quilt using Christmas ties. She was delighted, and we have named this quilt in honor of her father. This is a great way to use up all those Christmas fabric scraps.

Fabric Requirements

10 fat quarters of assorted medium/dark
    holiday prints for blocks A, B and C
1 fat quarter medium/dark holiday print for
    block D
10 fat quarters of assorted lights for blocks A,
    B and C
1 fat quarter light for block D
1 1/2 yards outer border fabric
3/4 yard for binding
4 yards for backing

Cutting Instructions

Assorted medium/dark fat quarters
1. Cut each fat quarter into 3 1/2" x 22" strips. You should have 50 strips.

2. Using five of these medium/dark strips, cut one strip into 2 – 3 1/2" x 9" rectangles; keep as pairs for block A. Cut another strip into 2 – 3 1/2" x 9" rectangles; keep as pairs for block B.

3. Cut the remaining strips into 60 – 3 1/2" x 9" rectangles for block C.

Medium/dark fat quarter
Cut into 4 – 5 1/2" squares and 8 – 2" squares for block D.

Assorted light fat quarters
1. Cut into 3 1/2" x 22" strips. You should have 50 strips.

2. Using five of these strips, cut one strip into 2 – 3 1/2" x 9 1/2" rectangles; keep as pairs for block A. Cut one strip into 2 – 3 1/2" x 9 1/2" rectangles; keep as pairs for block B.

3. Cut the remaining strips into 94 – 3 1/2" x 4" rectangles.

Light fat quarter
Cut into 8 – 5" squares and 4 – 5 1/2" squares for block D.

Outer border
Cut 8 – 6 1/2" x WOF strips

Binding
Cut 8 – 2 1/2" x WOF strips

Block A	Block B	Block C	Block D
Make 10	Make 10	Make 18	Make 4

Sewing Instructions
Block A

1. Draw a diagonal line on the reverse side of the 3 1/2" x 4" light rectangles, as shown.

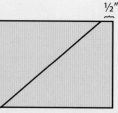

2. Place a light rectangle face down on a dark rectangle as shown. The light rectangle will overlap the dark rectangle by 1/2".

3. Sew on the drawn line. Flip open to make sure the pieces are sewn together correctly. Trim the seam to 1/4" and press toward the dark.

4. Repeat with the other matched set, but with the diagonal seam going in the opposite direction. Trim the seam and press toward the light.

5. Sew a light 3 1/2" x 9 1/2" rectangle to the left side of unit just completed. This piece should be the same light print as the 3 1/2" x 4" rectangle used in step 1. Press the seam toward the light fabric.

6. Make 10 of block A. Square to 9 1/2".

7. Join 5 A blocks end-to-end to make a vertical row that measures 9 1/2" x 45 1/2". Make sure the ties are all pointing in the same direction. Press seams toward the top.

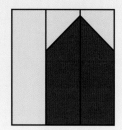

Block A

8. Make 2 rows. Label these Row 2 and Row 4.

Block B

1. Construct block B in the same manner as block A, but sew the light 3 1/2" x 9 1/2" rectangle to the right side of the unit. Press seam toward the light rectangle.

2. Make 10 of block B. Square to 9 1/2".

3. Join 5 B blocks end-to-end to make a vertical row that measures 9 1/2" x 45 1/2". Make sure the ties are all pointing in the same direction. Press seams toward the top.

4. Make 2 rows. Label these Row 3 and Row 5.

Marshall Field's former flagship store on State Street, in The Loop of downtown Chicago, was officially renamed "Macy's on State Street" on September 9, 2006. It is now the flagship store of Federated Department Stores' Macy's North Division and is one of three national flagship locations for Macy's

Block C

1. Using 54 - 3 1/2" x 9 1/2" assorted medium/dark rectangles and 54 - 3 1/2" x 4" light rectangles, sew a diagonal seam as in blocks A and B. Press seam toward the dark rectangle.

2. Randomly select 3 units and sew them together to create block C. Make sure the diagonals are all going in the same direction. Press seams all in one direction.

3. Join 4 C blocks together side-by-side to make a horizontal inner border that measures 9 1/2" x 36 1/2". Make 2, one for the top and one for the bottom. Press all seams in one direction. Label these as Row 7 and Row 8.

4. Join 5 C blocks together end-to-end to make a vertical side inner border that measures 9 1/2" x 45 1/2". Make 2, one for each side. Press all seams in one direction. Label these as Row 1 and Row 6.

Block D

This bow-tie block forms the four corners of the quilt.

Half-square Triangle Units
1. Using four 5 1/2" squares of light and four 5 1/2" squares of dark, lay the squares right sides together. Draw a diagonal line on the wrong side of the light square. Sew 1/4" on each side of the line.

2. Cut on the line and press open to reveal a half-square triangle unit. Square to 5". Make 8.

Corner Units
1. Draw a diagonal line on the wrong side of the 2" dark squares.

2. Place a dark 2" square right side down on one corner of a 5" light square. Sew on the drawn line. Fold back to check alignment of the corner. Trim the seam to 1/4" and press the square open. Make 8.

3. Join 2 half-square triangle units and 2 corner units to make a four-patch as shown in the block D diagram. Press the joining seams open to reduce bulk. Square to 9 1/2". Make 4.

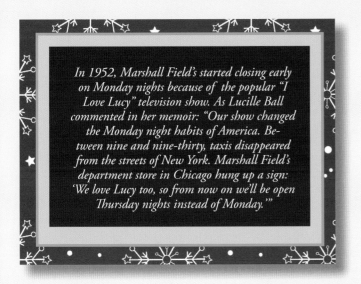

In 1952, Marshall Field's started closing early on Monday nights because of the popular "I Love Lucy" television show. As Lucille Ball commented in her memoir: "Our show changed the Monday night habits of America. Between nine and nine-thirty, taxis disappeared from the streets of New York. Marshall Field's department store in Chicago hung up a sign: 'We love Lucy too, so from now on we'll be open Thursday nights instead of Monday.'"

Make the Quilt

1. Starting with Row 1 on the left side (points facing out), lay out all of the rows in numerical order. Turn Row 6 so the points face out from the center of quilt.

2. Sew a block D to both ends of Rows 7 and 8. Be sure they are facing in the correct direction.
Turn Row 2 and Row 4 so the tie points are facing down. Rows 3 and 5 tie points should face up.

3. Sew Rows 1 through 6 together, matching seams and pressing.

4. Add Row 7 to the top of the quilt with the tie points facing up.

5. Sew Row 8 to the bottom of the quilt center with tie points facing down.

6. Sew the 6 1/2" outer border strips into one long strip using diagonal seams. Trim seams to 1/4" and press open.

7. Measure through the middle of the quilt vertically. Cut 2 side outer borders to this measurement and attach one to each side. Press seams toward borders.

8. Measure through the middle of the quilt horizontally. Cut the top and bottom outer borders to this measurement and attach to the top and bottom.

9. Quilt as desired and bind.

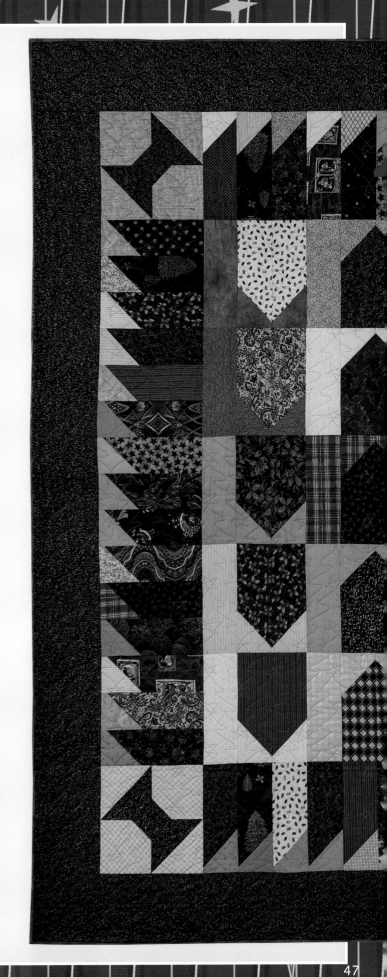

NOTES ON EMBROIDERY AND EMBROIDERY STITCHES

Here are a few notes and tips for completing the embroidery in this book. Further instructions are included with the block designs.

Layering with Muslin
The embroidered blocks should be created using a layer of muslin on the back of the fabric block. This ensures that the threads on the back of the block do not show through on the finished quilt. This also stabilizes the embroidery.

Design Transfer
For ease in transferring the designs, we recommend using a product such as Sulky Sticky Fabri-Solvy, available at most quilt shops. The standard-size sheets (8 1/2″ x 11″) are self-adhesive and repositionable, and they can be run through a printer. Simply peel the printed design from the backing paper and center it on the block. Place a hoop over all three layers (muslin, fabric and Fabri-Solvy) and stitch. When the entire pattern has been completed, remove the hoop and submerse the block in water according to the manufacturer's directions. The Fabri-Solvy will dissolve, leaving only the embroidery. This method saves time and has the added benefit of leaving no marks on the block that may not be covered by thread.

This product is also available in 20″ x 30″ sheets for use on the large center block of the Grand Tree Wall Hanging. While most printers cannot print on this size, the tracing is easily done directly on the product. After the design is traced, peel off the backing and place the Fabri-Solvy on the large block. We find that it is easier to trace on the Fabri-Solvy than the fabric.

Floss Colors and Strand Count
The DMC color and the number of strands to use are indicated for every embroidery pattern. DMC cotton embroidery floss was used for most of the projects. However, we recommend using metallic thread along with the cotton floss to embellish some designs. Metallic thread for machine sewing, such as Sulky, is the best for this as it does not shred easily and lays beautifully in the design. While the cost is a bit more, there is less wasted thread and the results are worth the expense.

Embroidered Blocks
After the Fabri-Solvy has been removed, dry the blocks and press them from the back side. Square the finished block to the size given in the instructions.

Embellishing the tree

The Great Tree is decorated with crystal bicone AB beads, sizes 4mm (50), 2.5 mm (40) and 2mm (40). These should be sewn on AFTER the quilting is complete. Using mono-filament thread, carefully attach the beads making sure you stitch into the quilt batting. The larger 4mm beads should be attached to the bottom half of the tree, the 2.5mm beads should be stitched about one-third of the way up (mixed and blended with the 4mm), with the tiny 2 mm beads stitched to the top portion. It is best to knot the thread to secure each bead. This will prevent all of the beads from coming off in case one bead is snagged. Do not cut the thread after the knot of each bead. Simply bury the needle in the batting and come up through the top where the next bead will be stitched.

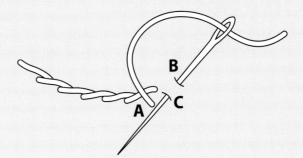

Stem Stitch

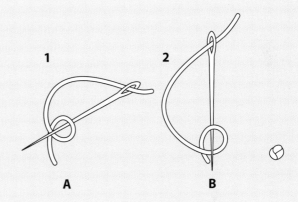

French Knot

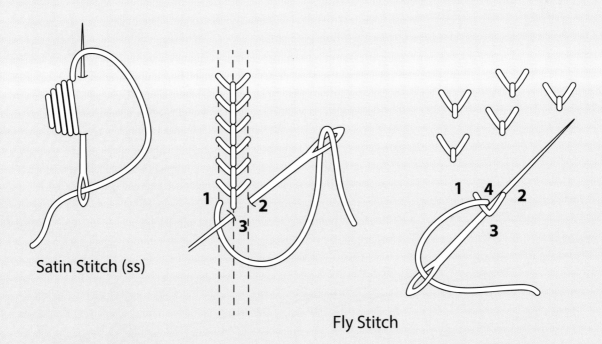

Satin Stitch (ss)

Fly Stitch

49

EMBROIDERY DESIGNS AND PATTERNS

All embroidery is done using 2 strands of floss and the outline stitch, unless otherwise noted.

Grand Tree Floss Guide

DMC 890 Ultra Dark Pistachio Green
    Tree: fly stitch (only trace branch lines, then fill in needles with fly stitch)
DMC 842 Very Light Beige Brown
    Vertical building columns
DMC 839 Dark Beige Brown
    Dark horizontal balcony molding
DMC 434 Very Light Golden Olive
    Alternate horizontal balcony molding
DMC 840 Medium Beige Brown
    Horizonal trim
DMC 841 Light Beige Brown
    Horizontal trim
Copper Metallic
    Windowpane squares (1 strand)
    Star shapes on balcony rail
Embellish with crystal bicone bead, etc., AFTER quilting.

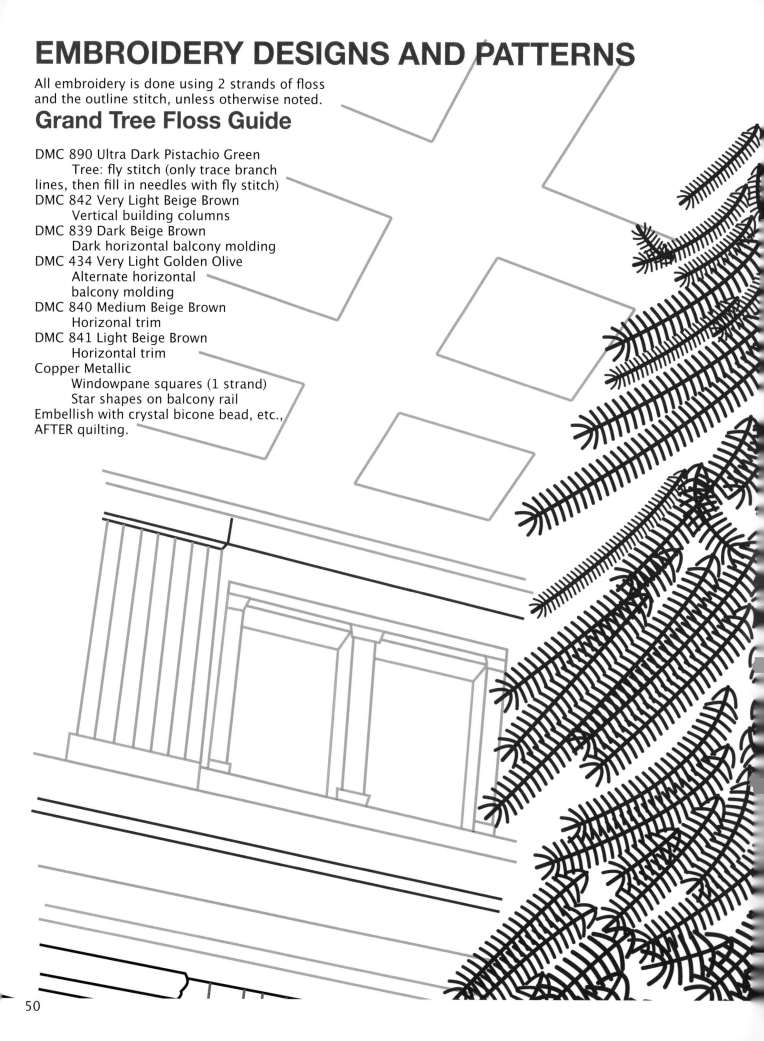

Diamond Ring

Christmas Window Quilt Block A

"Give the Lady What She Wants" was quite the marketing strategy, especially when it came to the jewelry department. My father was a watchmaker in a jewelry store, and every Christmas morning my mother would receive a sparkling token from Santa.

DMC 796
  Ring box outline: 2 strands, outline stitch
  Ring box outside: 3 strands, satin stitch
DMC 157
  Ring box lid side lining: 3 strands, satin stitch
DMC 890
  Evergreen boughs: 2 strands, fly stitch
  Gift tag outline and strings: 2 strands, outline stitch
DMC 782
  Necklace links: 2 strands, outline stitch
DMC 816
  Heart: 2 strands, satin stitch (add ruby faceted bead after quilting)
DMC 436
  2 Carats Tag: 2 strands, outline stitch

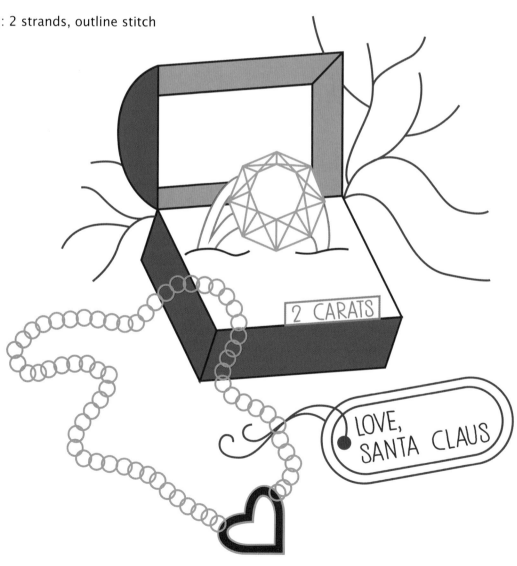

Ring In the New Year

Christmas Window Quilt Block B

Marshall Field's had an extensive gourmet shop featuring a vast selection of fine wines. The shop was very busy during the holidays, especially in the days leading up to New Year's Eve. I rarely see anything in the quilting world referencing New Year's, so I wanted to include this block.

DMC 890
    Bottle: 2 strands, outline stitch
    Bottom of bottle: 3 strands, satin stitch
DMC 729
    Watch case: 2 strands, outline stitch
DMC 816
    Horizontal stripes on bottle: 3 strands, satin stitch
DMC 310
    Hands: 2 strands, satin stitch

    Numerals: 2 strands, outline stitch
    GW Gullic Watchmaker: 2 strands, outline stitch
DMC 796
    Champagne letters/bottle ribbon: 2 strands, outline stitch
DMC 907
    Happy New Year: 1 strand 907 + 1 strand gold metallic, outline stitch
Ribbon Streamers:
    DMC 796, 155, 718, 550, 165, 703. Use 2 strands of each, satin stitch
Gold Metallic
Silver Metallic
    Background stars: 2 strands, single stitches

Holiday Stockings

Christmas Window Quilt Block C

We all had Christmas socks made by my grandmother,
and it was such fun to empty the trinkets and candy out
of them on Christmas morning.

DMC 817
> Outline cuff points: 2 strands, outline stitch
> Stripes: 2 strands, chain stitch

DMC 909
> Outline sock and plaid lines in one direction: 2
> strands, outline stitch

DMC 729
> Outline bows: 2 strands, outline stitch
> Bow opening and ribbon tails: 2 strands, satin
> stitch
> Outline plaid lines in other direction: 2 strands,
> outline stitch

Gold Metallic
> Outline bells: 2 strands outline stitch, French
> knots

Uncle Mistletoe

Christmas Window Quilt Block D

Uncle Mistletoe and Aunt Holly were popular assistants in the Cottage where we visited Santa. Their images were featured in the windows and on the Great Tree.

DMC 890
> Mittens: 2 strands, outline stitch
> Scarf border: 2 strands, satin stitch
> Dots on scarf: 2 strands, French knots
> Holly leaves on pockets: 1 strand, outline stitch

DMC 168
> Hair: 3 strands, satin stitch

DMC 310
> Hat and face outline: 2 strands, outline stitch
> Eyebrows and shoes: 2 strands, satin stitch

DMC 817
> Coat/scarf/pockets outline: 2 strands, outline stitch
> Hatband, trim on pockets and cape, cuffs and coat hem: 3 strands, satin stitch
> Holly berries on pockets: 1 strand, French knots

DMC 471
> Mistletoe sprig on hat: 2 strands, satin stitch

DMC 3865
> Mistletoe berries on hat: 2 strands, French knots

Silver Metallic
> Wings: 2 strands, outline stitch

Lightly rub pale pink tint on cheeks

Big Clock

Christmas Window Quilt Block E

This is perhaps the best-known icon of the Marshall Field's store.

DMC 890
    2 strands, outline stitch all EXCEPT
Clock Hands
    2 strands, black satin stitch
Tips of clock frame/shaded areas of clock
    2 strands DMC 3813 + 1 strand copper metallic, satin stitch
Outlines on clock indicated on pattern
    2 strands DMC 3813 + 1 strand copper metallic, outline stitch

Marshall Field's Bag

Christmas Window Quilt Block F

Busy shoppers were seen everywhere carrying Marshall Field's shopping bags loaded with gifts.

DMC 816
> Square box: 2 strands, outline stitch for lines in one direction on Plaid gift wrap roll: 2 strands, outline stitch
> Center box outline: 2 strands, outline stitch

DMC 820
> Dotted gift wrap roll outline: 2 strands, outline stitch
> Roll end: 2 strands, satin stitch
> Half of the dots: 2 strands, satin stitch

DMC 909
> Plaid gift wrap roll outline and plaid lines in opposite direction: 2 strands + 1 strand green metallic, outline stitch
> Roll end: 2 strands, satin stitch
> Ribbon and bow on left box: 2 strands + 1 strand metallic green, satin stitch

DMC 817
> Candy canes outline: 2 strands, outline stitch
> Candy cane stripes: 2 strands, satin stitch

DMC 890
> Bag outline and tree: 2 strands, outline stitch

DMC 676
> Ribbon on pack age next to candy canes: 2 strands + 1 strand gold metallic, satin stitch

DMC 167
> Dots on gift wrap roll: 2 strands + 1 strand silver metallic, satin stitch

DMC 600
> ` Outline package next to candy canes: 2 strands, outline stitch

Gold Metallic
> Marshall Field's logo and   star on tree: 2 strands outline stitch

Silver Metallic
> Left box outline: 2 strands, outline stitch

Multicolor Metallic
> Center box ribbon: 2 strands, satin stitch
> Center box curly bow: 2 strands, outline stitch

Candy Canes

Christmas Window Quilt Block G

Big candy canes were hung from the columns in the
Toy Department. We liked to believe they were real
candy.

DMC 796
    Bow openings: 3 strands, satin stitch
    Bow outline: 2 strands, outline stitch
    Bow dots: 1 strand + 1 strand silver metallic,
French knots
DMC 890
    Evergreen boughs: 2 strands, fly stitch
DMC 909
    Holly outline: 2
    strands, outline
stitch
DMC 817
    Holly berries: 2
    strands, French
    knots
DMC 902
    Candy cane
    outline:
    2 strands,
    outline stitch
    Stripes: 3
    strands, satin
    stitch

Silver Bells

Christmas Window Quilt Block H

I remember big silver bells hanging from the streetlights on State Street and often heard my grandma humming the song as we walked back to the train.

DMC 310
Silver bells and music: 1 strand + 1 strand silver metallic, outline stitch
DMC 410
Outline bells: 2 strands, outline stitch
Stripes on bells and clangers: 2 strands + 1 strand silver metallic, satin stitch
DMC 890
Evergreen boughs: 2 strands, fly stitch
DMC 902
Bow outline: 2 strands, outline stitch
Bow openings: 3 strands, satin stitch
Bow dots: 1 strand + 1 strand silver metallic, French knots

Frango Mints

Christmas Window Quilt Block I

These delicious melt-in-your-mouth chocolate candies are still a must-have at Christmas.

DMC 890
> Outline box: 2 strands, outline stitch
> Marshall Field's: 1 strand, outline stitch; 1 strand, French knot
> Frango: 2 strands + 1 strand green metallic, satin stitch
> Stripes: 3 strands + 1 strand green metallic, satin stitch
> *Alternate the direction of the satin stitch on the box stripes

DMC 503
> Stripes: 3 strands, satin stitch
> Leaves in the O of Frango: 2 strands, fly stitch leaf

DMC 3021
> Mint chocolates: 1 strand, outline stitch and French knot

Snow Globe

Christmas Window Quilt Block J

I remember all the big beautiful snow globes that decorated everyone's home during the holidays. They were so fun to shake as a child. Even today, isn't it hard to see one and not want to shake it?

DMC 890
   Tree: 2 strands, fly stitch
DMC 780
   Band at top of base: 2 strands + 1 strand copper metallic, satin stitch
DMC 898
   Base outline: 2 strands, outline stitch

DMC 892
   Horizontal accent line on base: 1 strand + 1 strand DMC 898, stem stitch
Silver Metallic
   Globe outline: 2 strands, outline stitch

Snowflakes: iridescent beads stitched on with clear monofilament thread AFTER quilting.

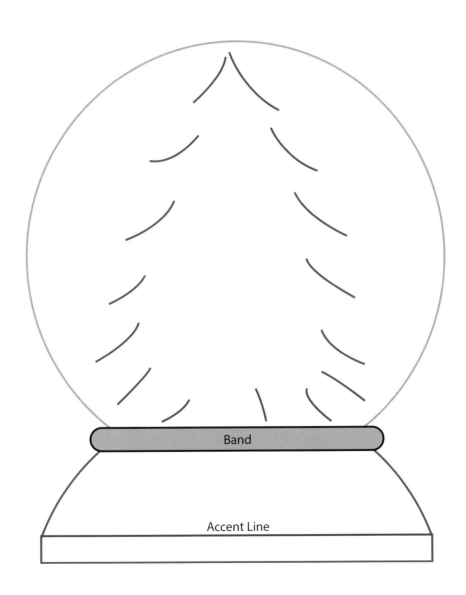

Band

Accent Line

Give the Lady What She Wants
Christmas Window Quilt Block K and Ornament Pillow

Noel Pole

Christmas Window Quilt Corner Stones

DMC Floss
Silver metallic
Copper metallic
816
890
310 for street names

RANDOLPH ST.

STATE ST.

WABASH AVE.

WASHINGTON ST.

STATE ST.

WASHINGTON ST.

RANDOLPH ST.

WABASH AVE.

Left Upper
Cornerstone

Left Lower
Cornerstone

Right Upper
Cornerstone

Right Lower
Cornerstone

Packages Appliqué

Christmas Window Quilt Block L

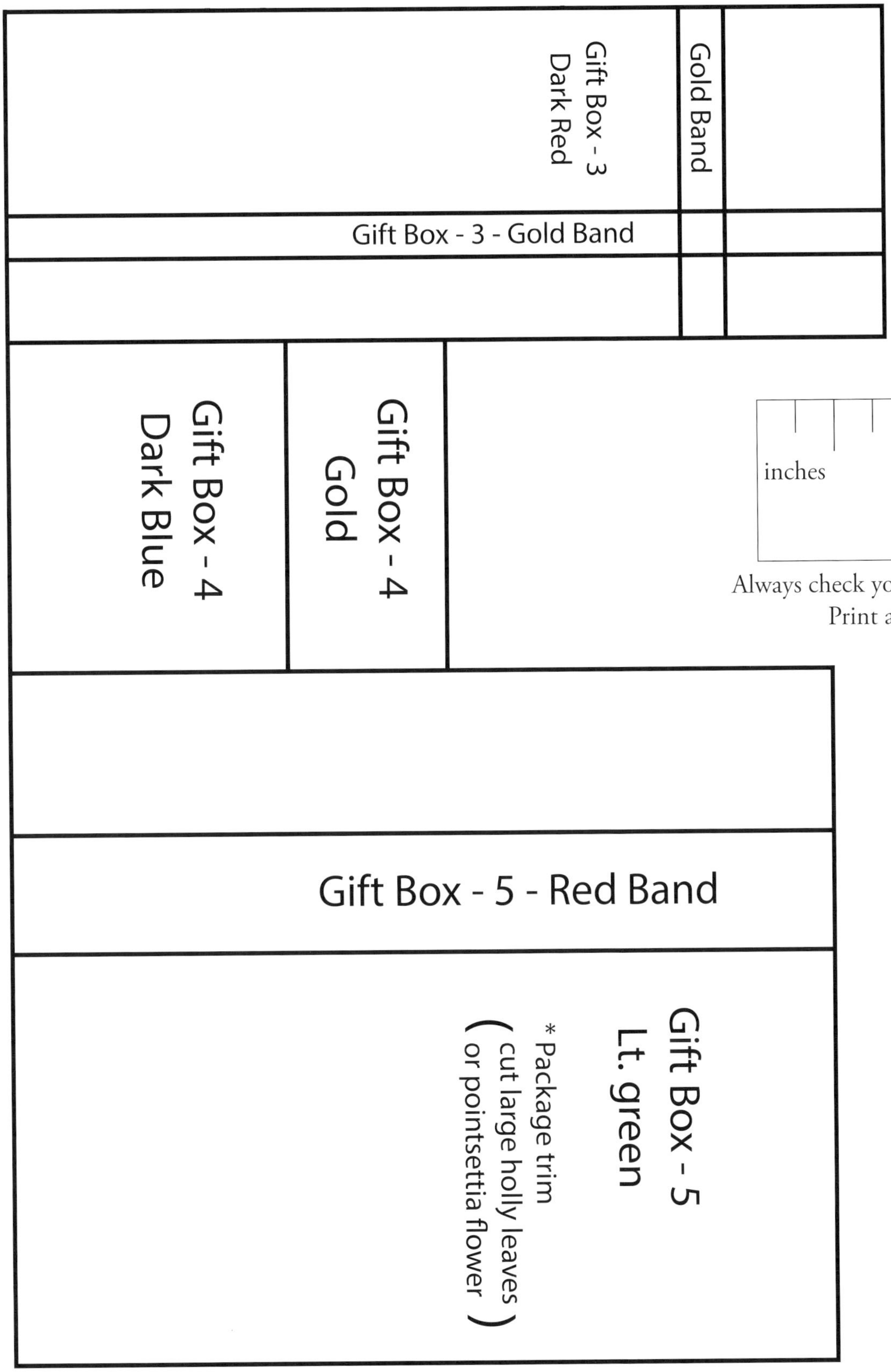

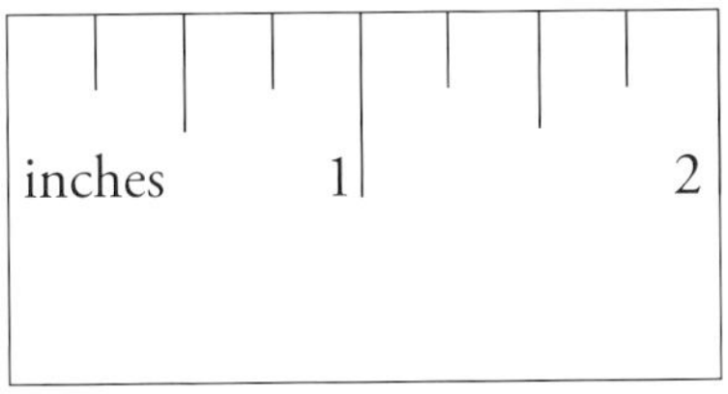

Gift Box - 3
Dark Red

Gold Band

Gift Box - 3 - Gold Band

Gift Box - 4
Dark Blue

Gift Box - 4
Gold

inches   1   2

Always check your print for correct size.
Print at 100 percent.

Gift Box - 5 - Red Band

Gift Box - 5
Lt. green

*Package trim
(cut large holly leaves
or pointsettia flower)

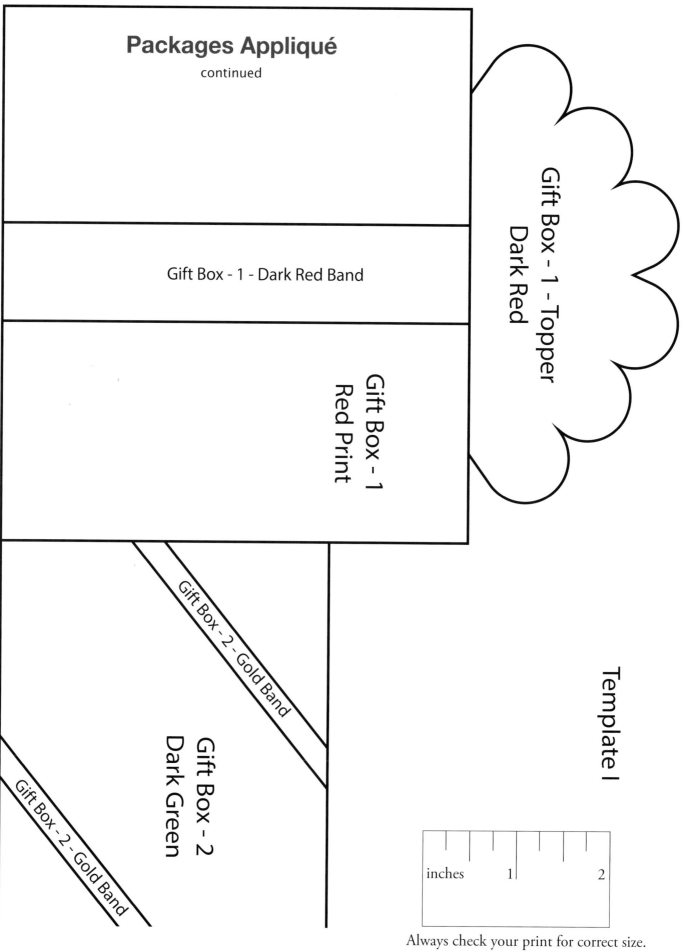

Packages Appliqué

continued

Gift Box - 1 - Dark Red Band

Gift Box - 1
Red Print

Gift Box - 1 - Topper
Dark Red

Gift Box - 2 - Gold Band

Gift Box - 2
Dark Green

Gift Box - 2 - Gold Band

Template I

inches 1 2

Always check your print for correct size.
Print at 100 percent.

Holiday Banner

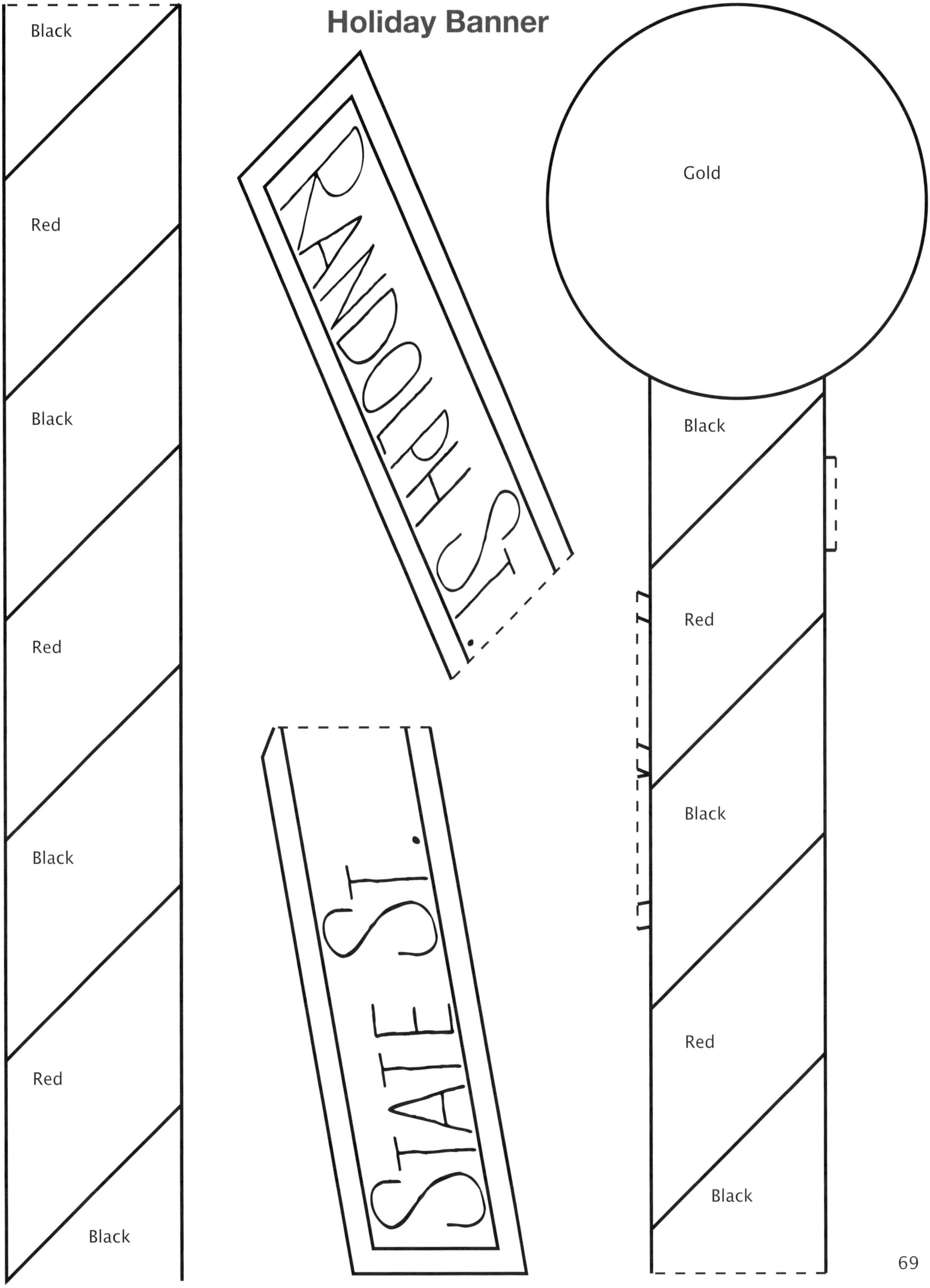

Black

Red

Black

Red

Black

Red

Black

RANDOLPH ST

STATE ST.

Gold

Black

Red

Black

Red

Black

inches 1 2

Always check your print for correct size.
Print at 100 percent.

Top to Bottom Tree Skirt

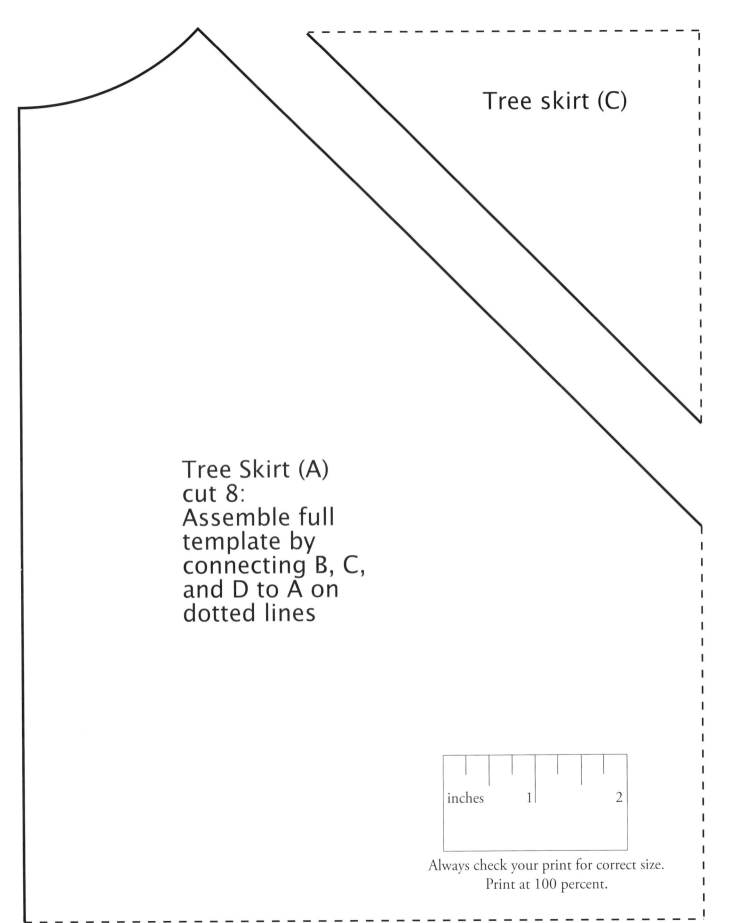

Tree skirt (C)

Tree Skirt (A)
cut 8:
Assemble full
template by
connecting B, C,
and D to A on
dotted lines

inches   1   2

Always check your print for correct size.
Print at 100 percent.

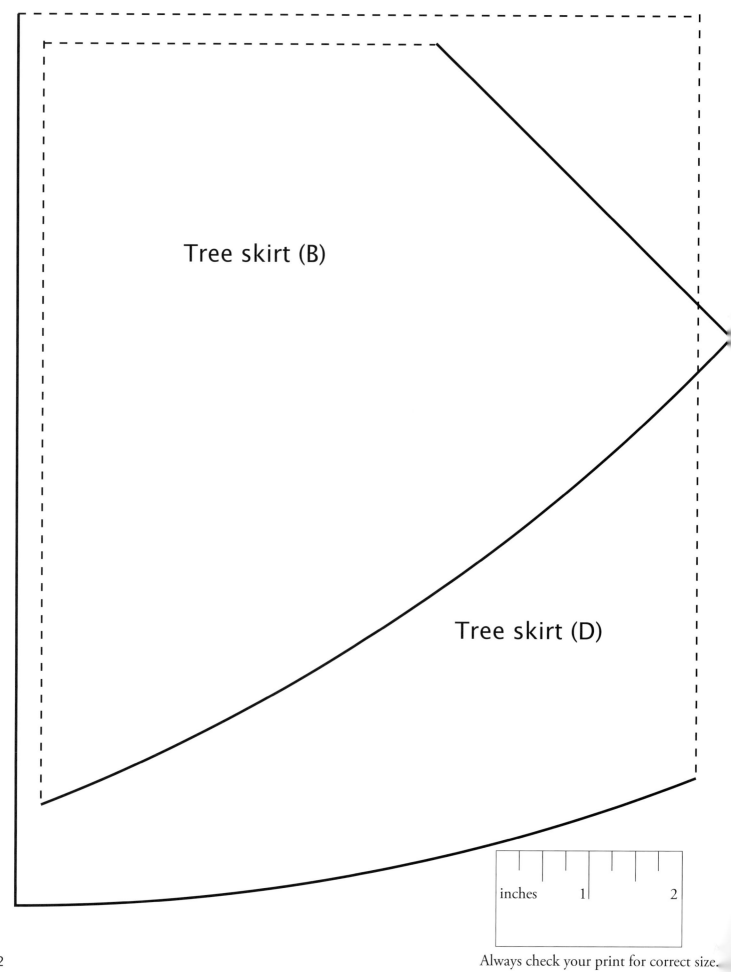

Tree skirt (B)

Tree skirt (D)

inches   1   2

Always check your print for correct size.
Print at 100 percent.

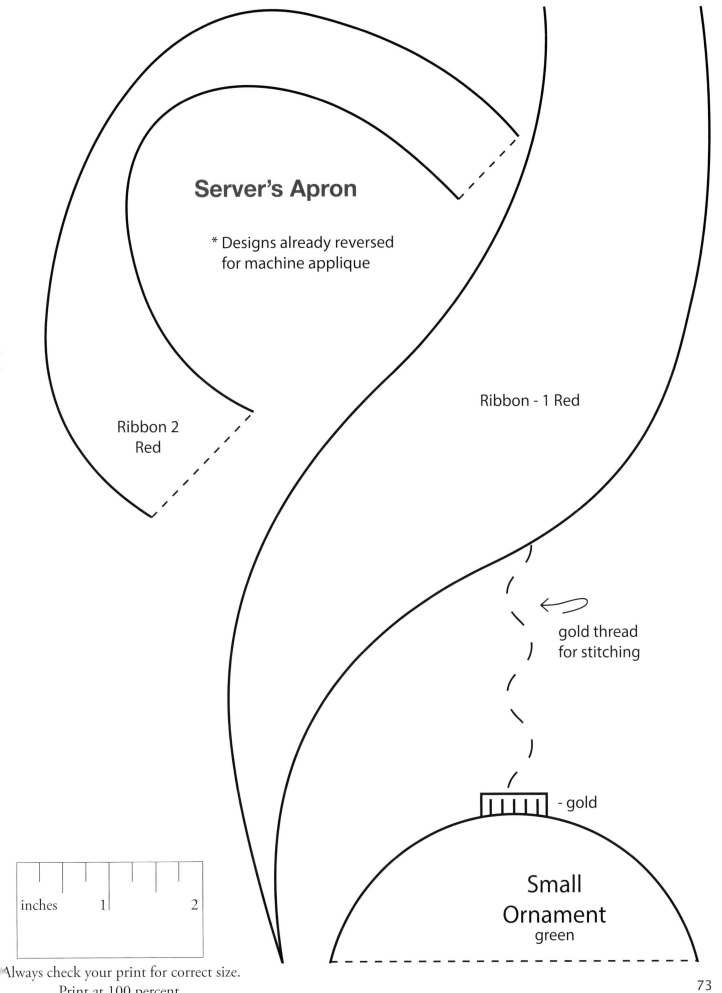

Server's Apron

* Designs already reversed
for machine applique

Ribbon 2
Red

Ribbon - 1 Red

gold thread
for stitching

- gold

Small
Ornament
green

inches 1 2

Always check your print for correct size.
Print at 100 percent.

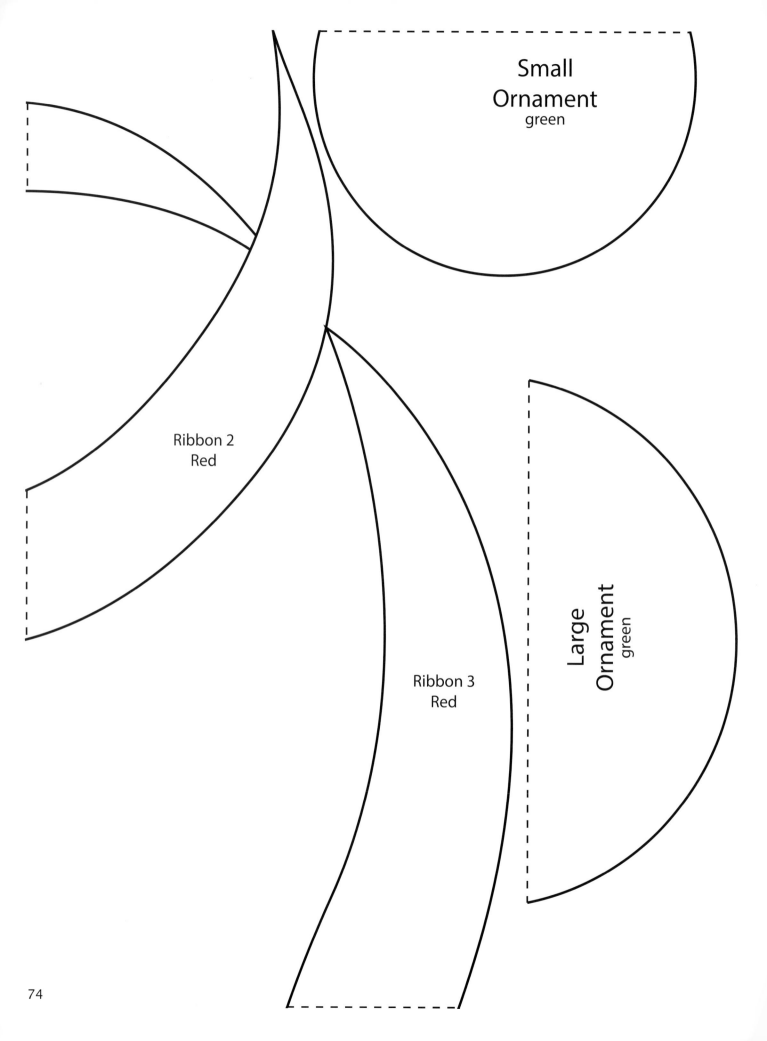

Small
Ornament
green

Ribbon 2
Red

Ribbon 3
Red

Large
Ornament
green

74

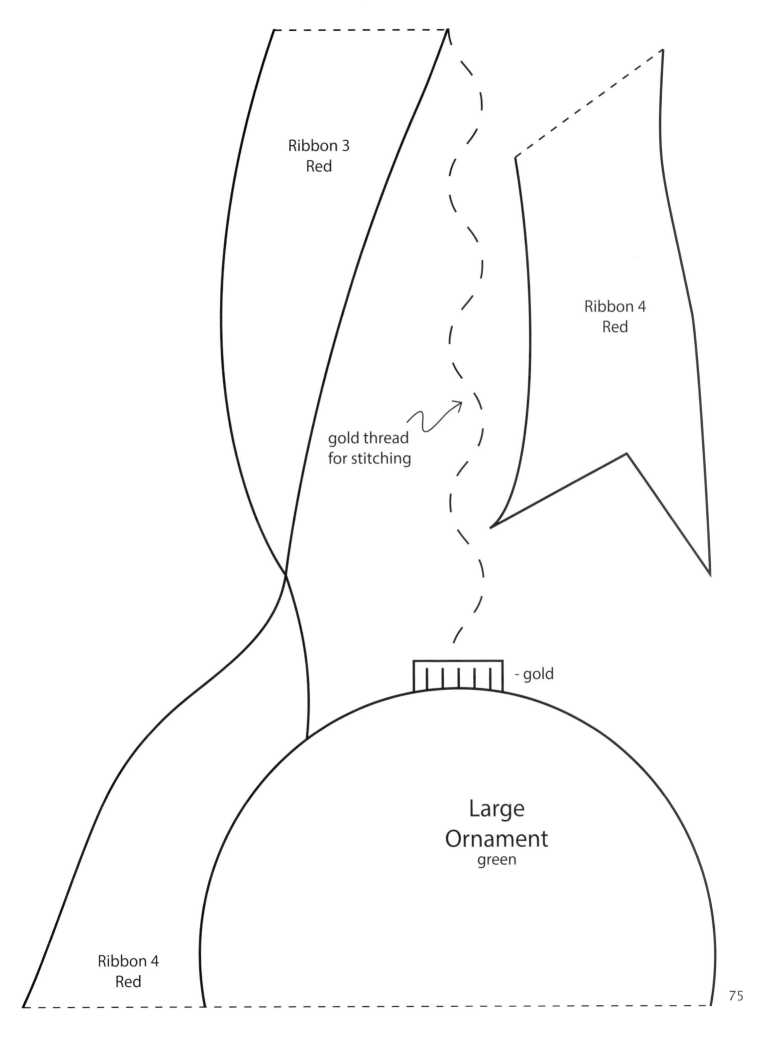

Ribbon 3
Red

Ribbon 4
Red

gold thread
for stitching

- gold

Large
Ornament
green

Ribbon 4
Red

75

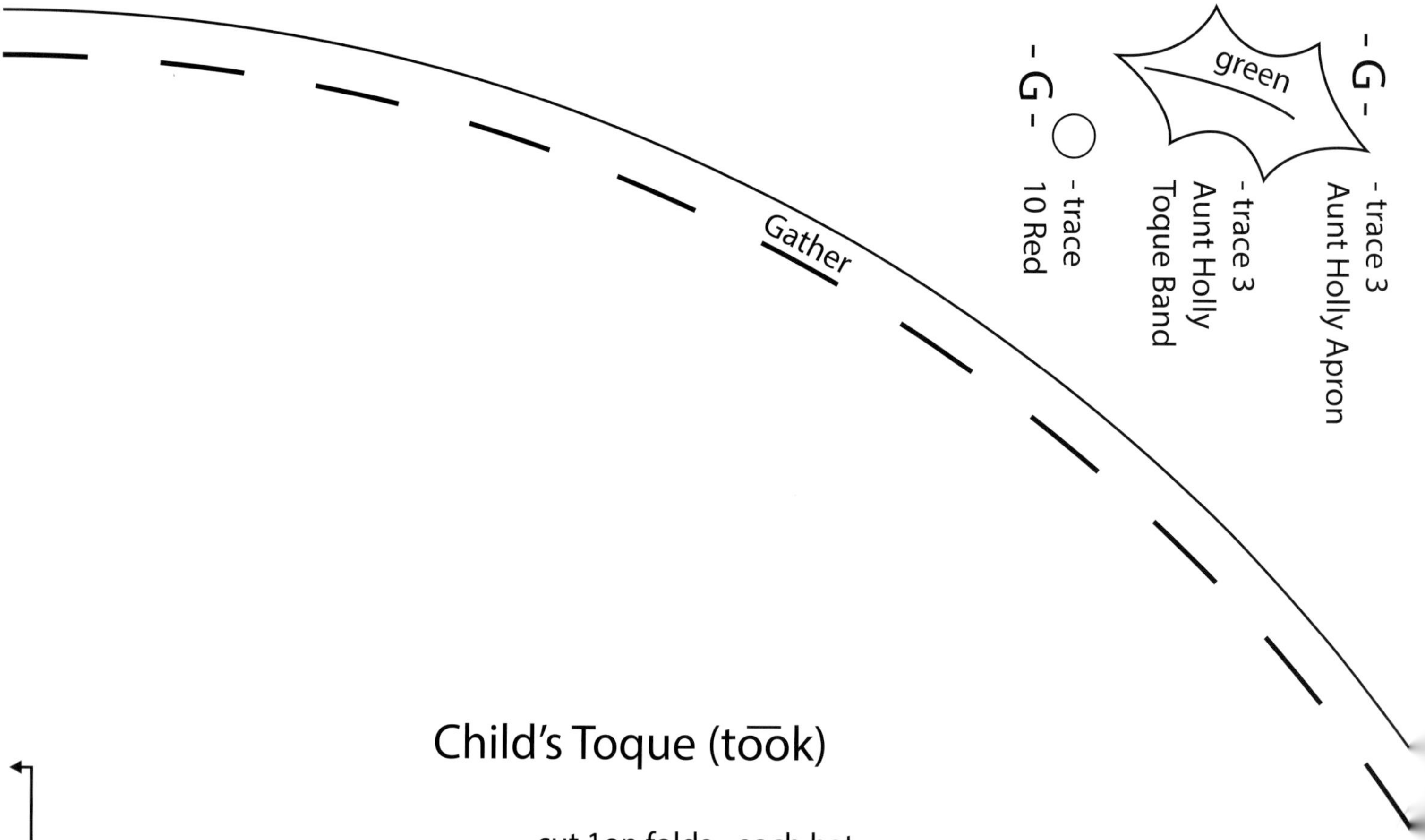

Gather

- G -
- G -
green

- trace 3
Aunt Holly Apron

- trace 3
Aunt Holly
Toque Band

- trace
10 Red

Child's Toque (to͞ok)

cut 1 on folds - each hat

Template E

Fold

Fold

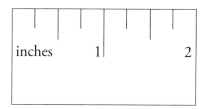

inches   1   2

Always check your print for correct size.
Print at 100 percent.

- F -
- trace 5
Uncle Mistletoe
- Toque Band -

Apron - Scarf Right

trace 1 - white

- F -

Apron - Scarf Left

trace 1 - white

- F -

Attach to
Template E
to create
circle

Apron - Pocket

white { cut 2
cut 2 reversed
Seam allow. included

- F -

green trim band

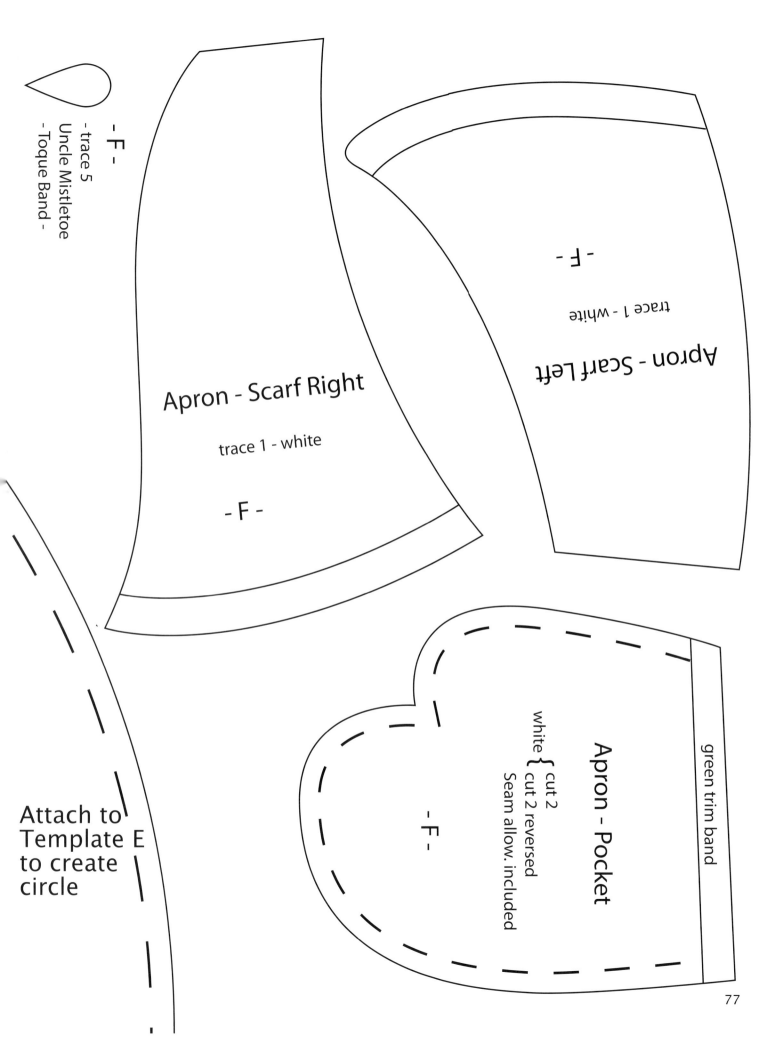

Children's Aprons

continued

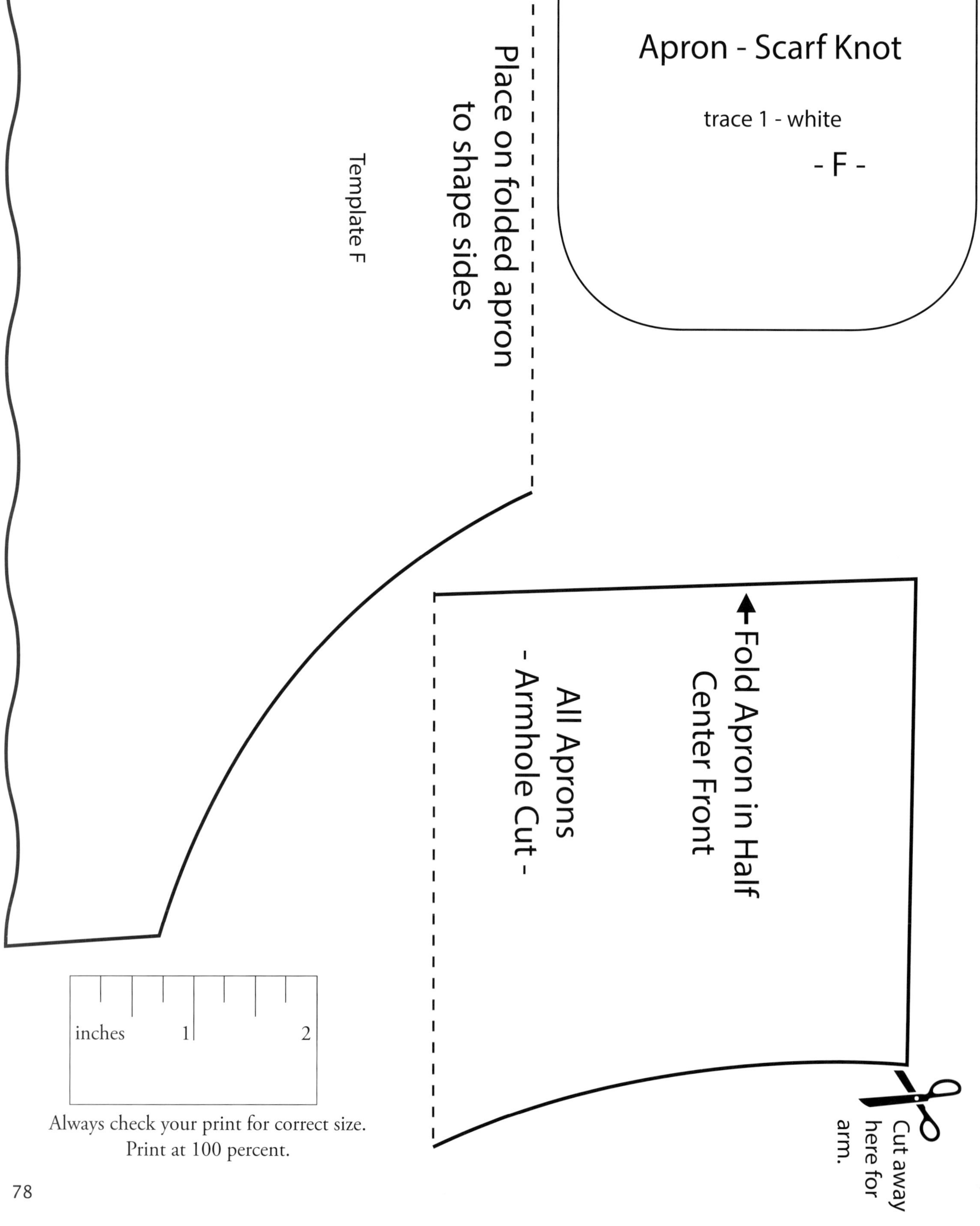

Place on folded apron
to shape sides

Template F

top ↑

Apron - Scarf Knot

trace 1 - white

- F -

Fold Apron in Half
Center Front ↑

All Aprons
- Armhole Cut -

inches   1   2

Always check your print for correct size.
Print at 100 percent.

Cut away
here for
arm.

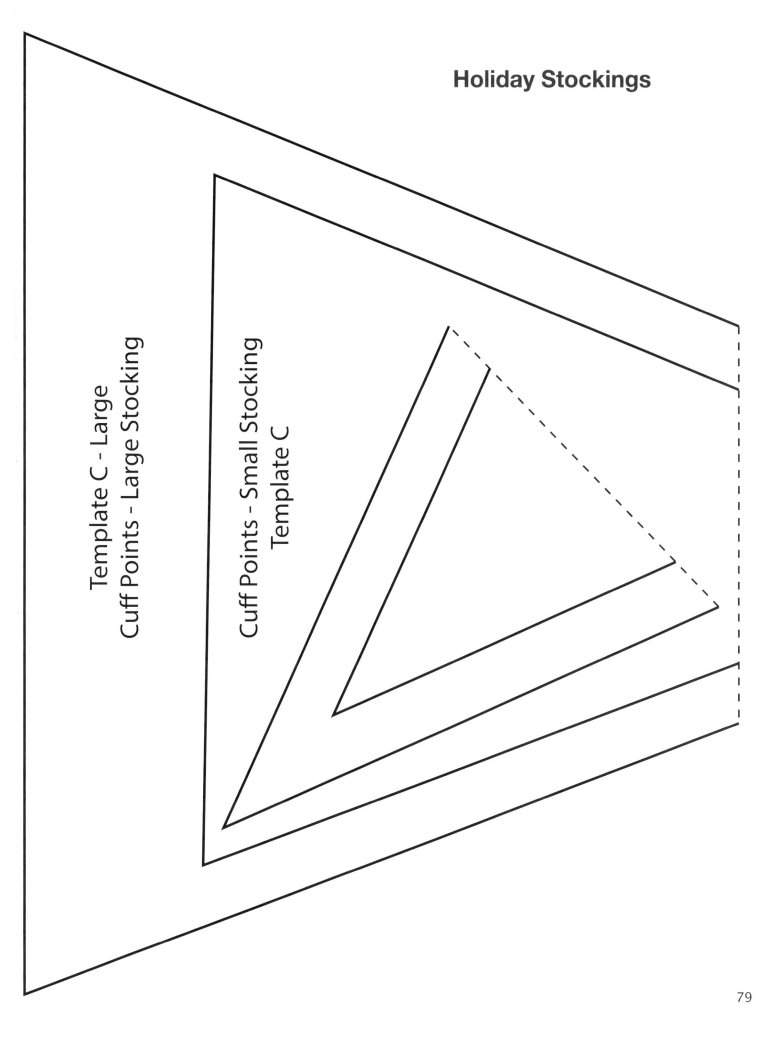

Template C - Large
Cuff Points - Large Stocking

Cuff Points - Small Stocking
Template C

Holiday Stockings
Large stocking continued

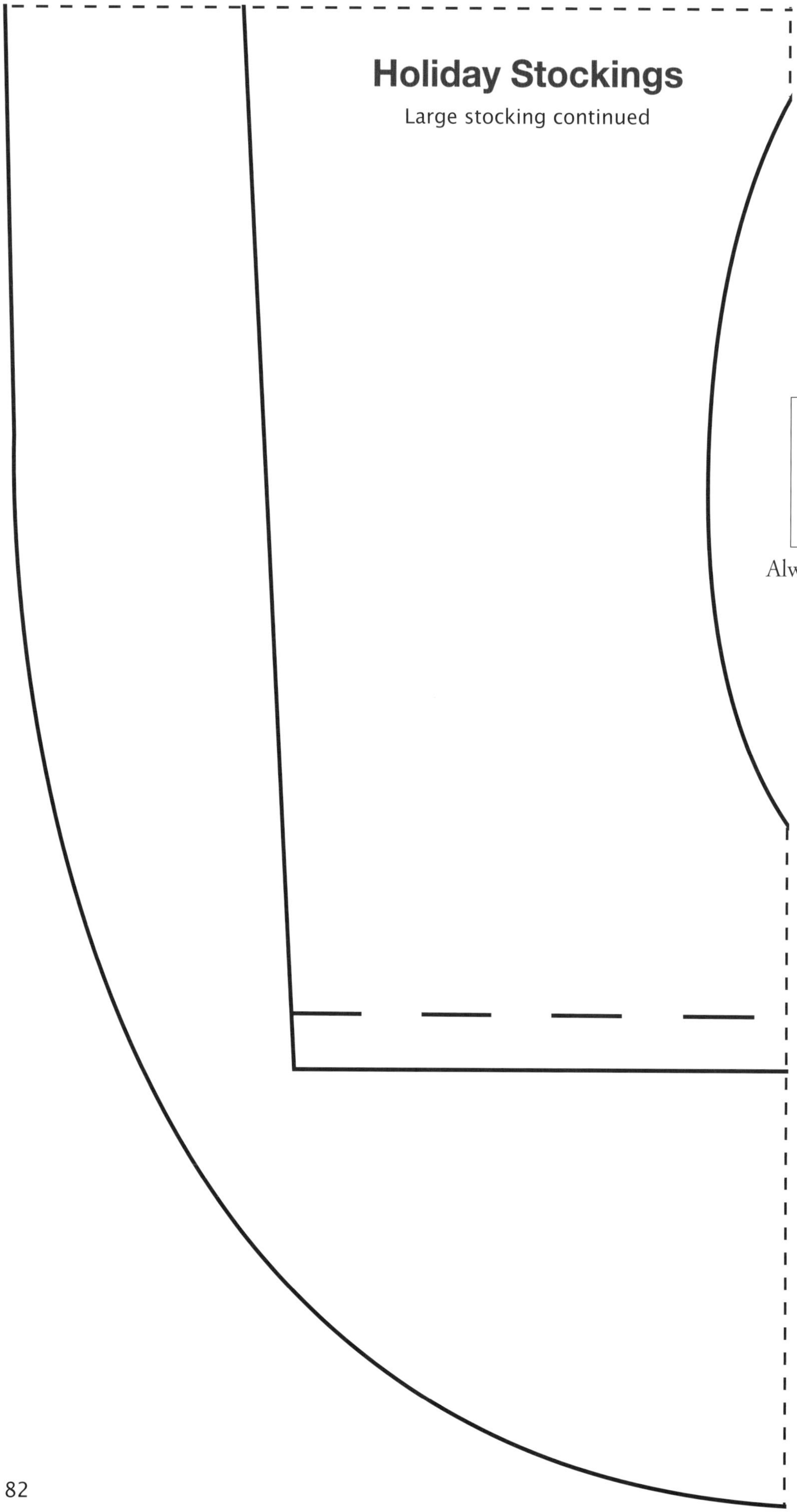

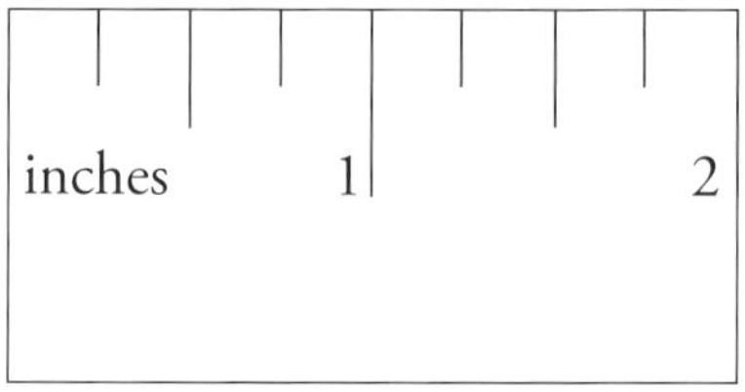

inches 1 2

Always check your print for correct size.
Print at 100 percent.

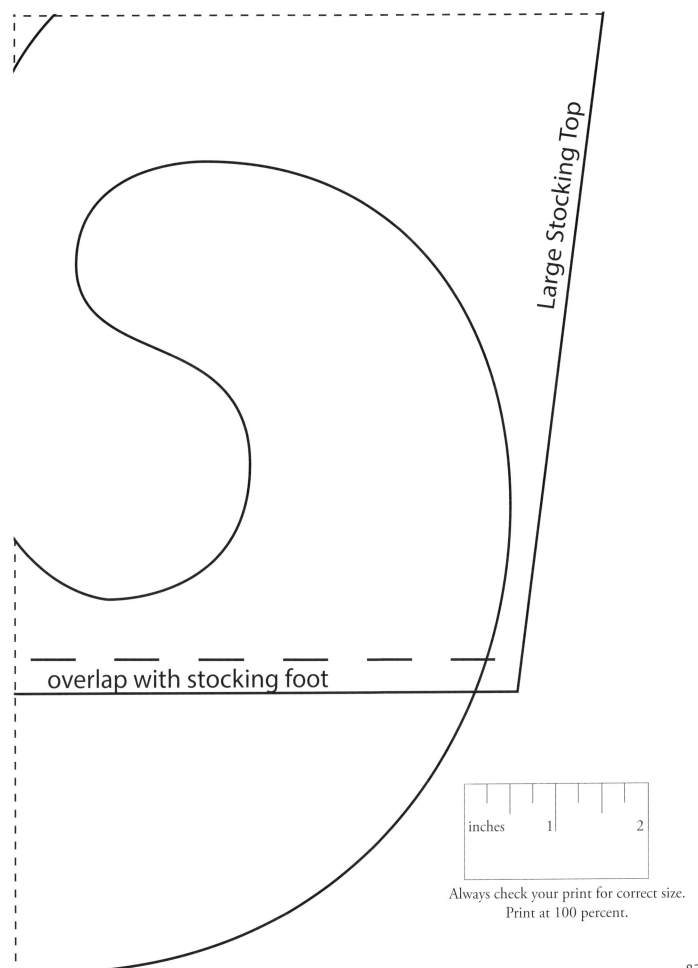

Large Stocking Top

overlap with stocking foot

inches 1 2

Always check your print for correct size.
Print at 100 percent.

83

Small Stocking

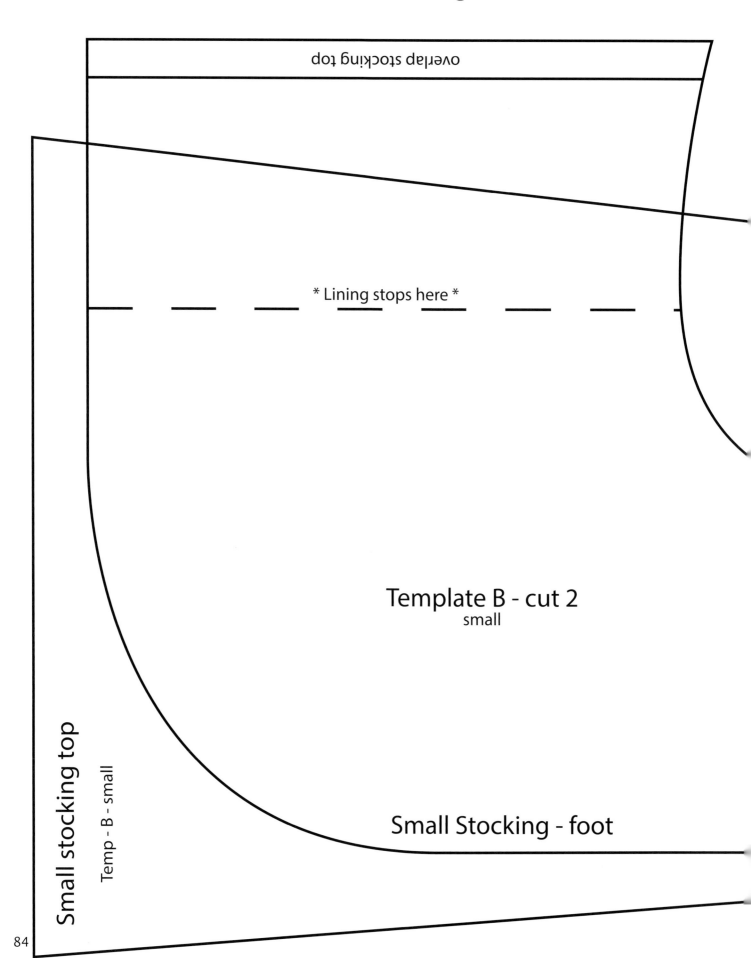

overlap stocking top

* Lining stops here *

Template B - cut 2
small

Small stocking top

Temp - B - small

Small Stocking - foot

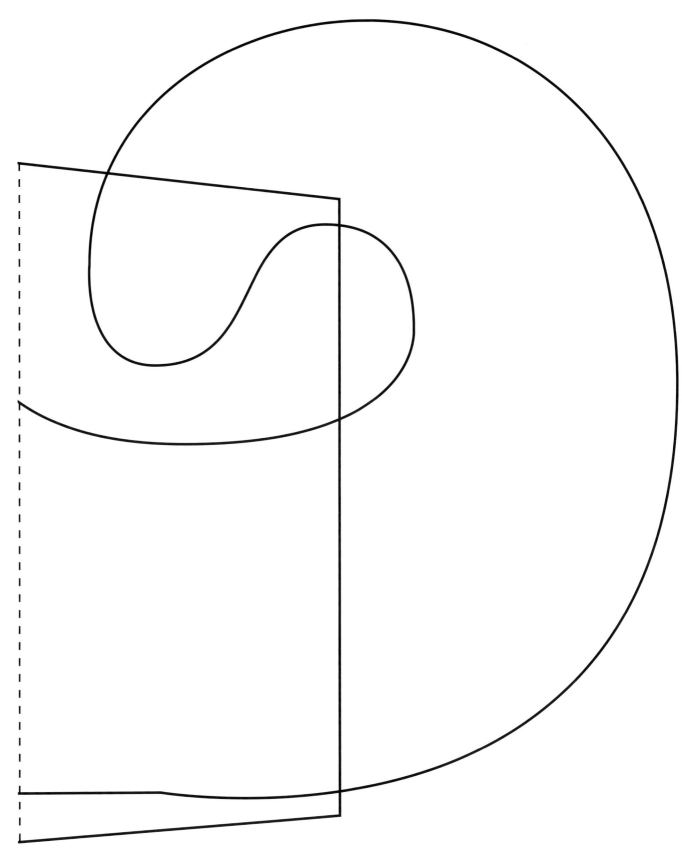

Placemats, Tea Cozy and Holiday Tote Bag

inches   1   2

Always check your print for correct size.
Print at 100 percent.

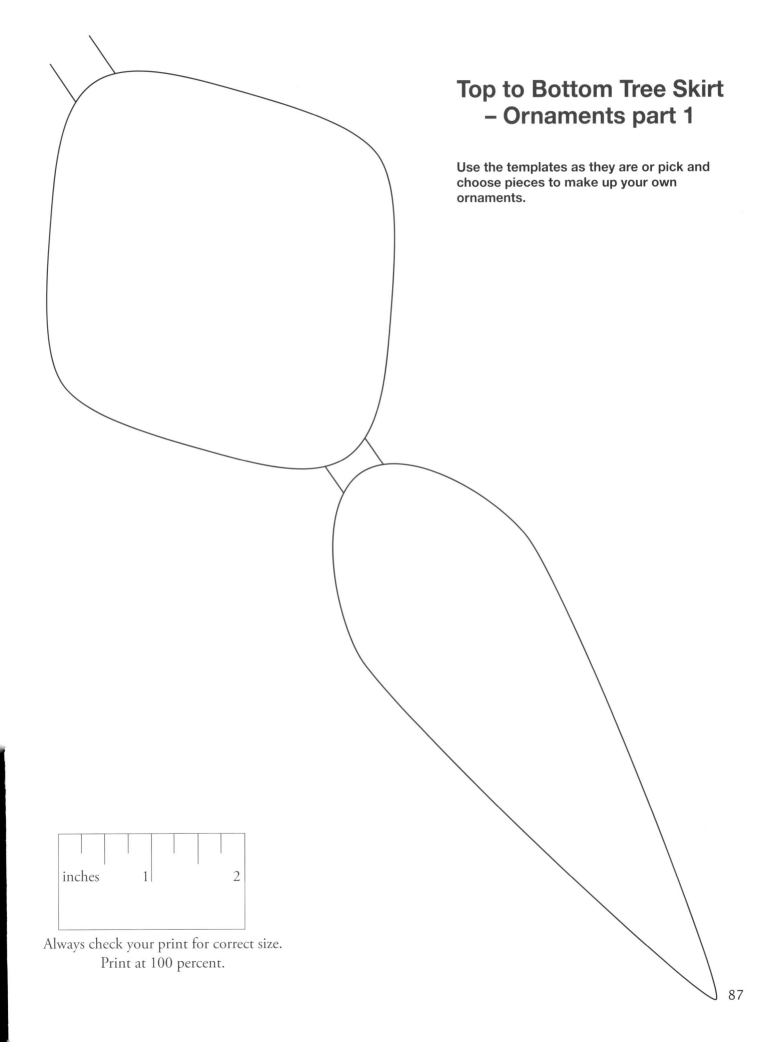

Top to Bottom Tree Skirt
– Ornaments part 1

Use the templates as they are or pick and choose pieces to make up your own ornaments.

inches   1   2

Always check your print for correct size.
Print at 100 percent.

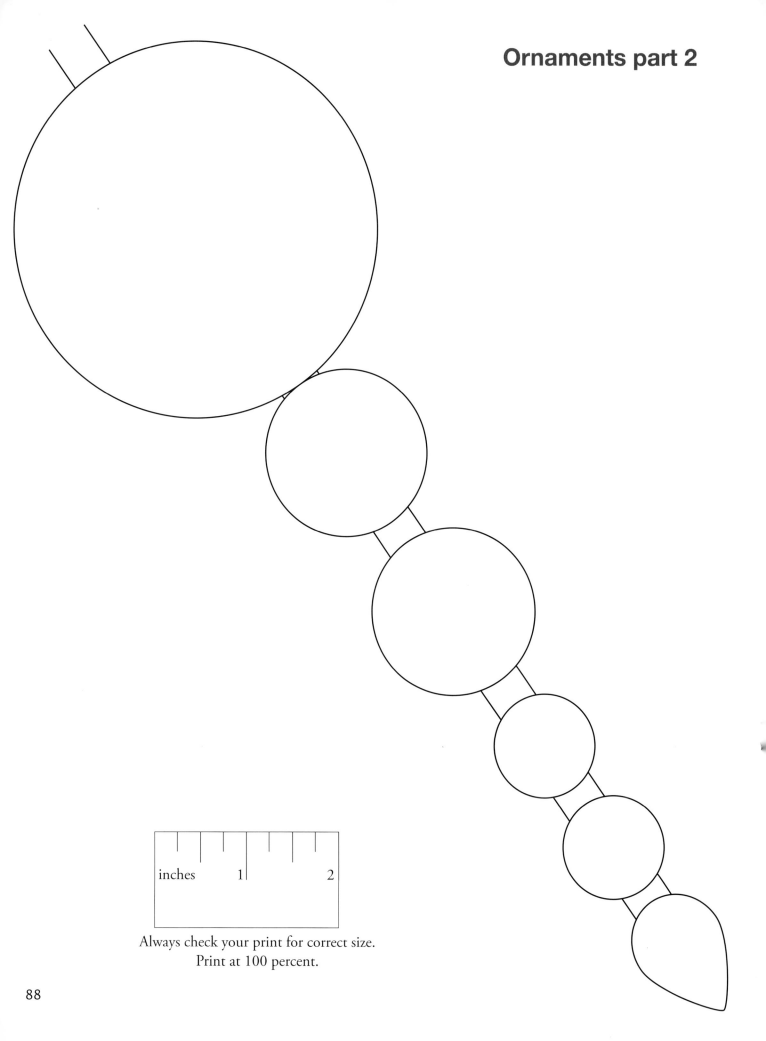

Ornaments part 2

inches   1   2

Always check your print for correct size.
Print at 100 percent.

88

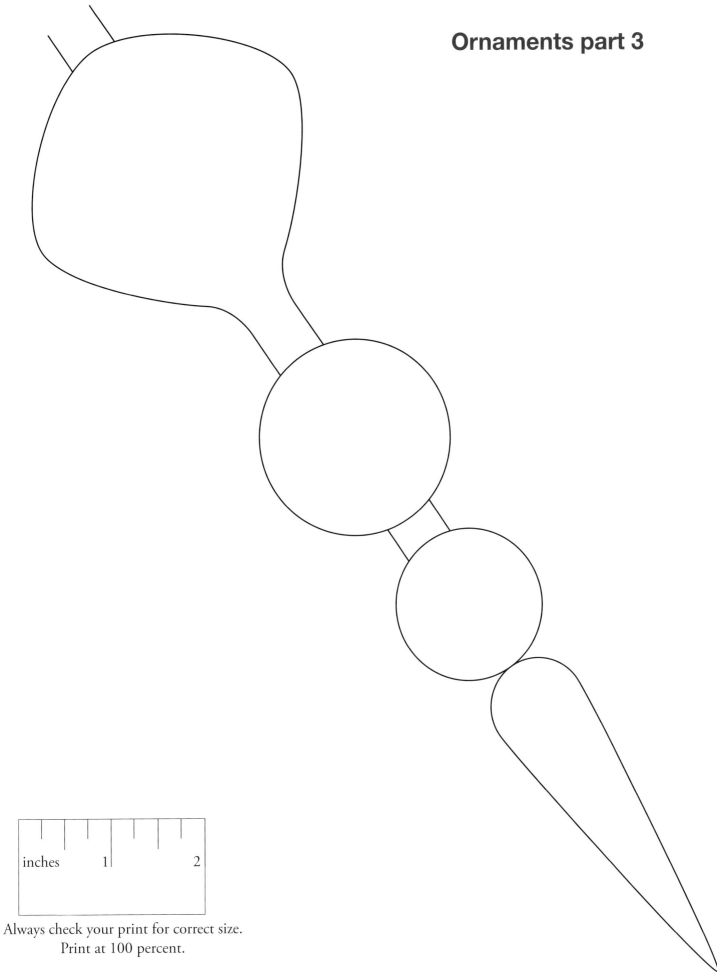

inches   1   2

Always check your print for correct size.
Print at 100 percent.

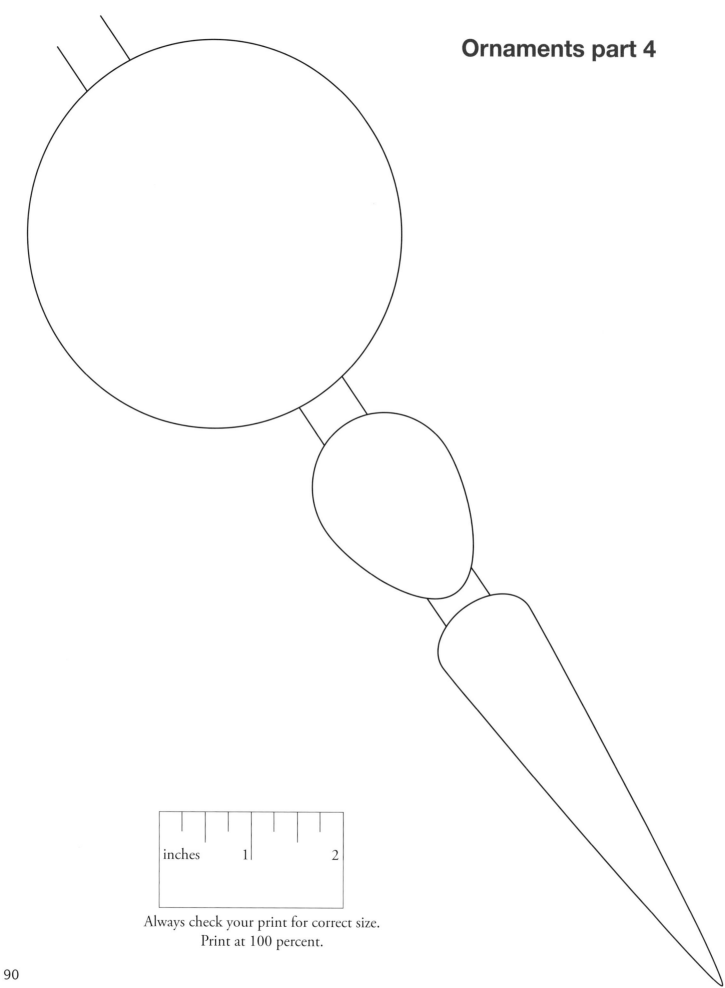

inches   1   2

Always check your print for correct size.
Print at 100 percent.

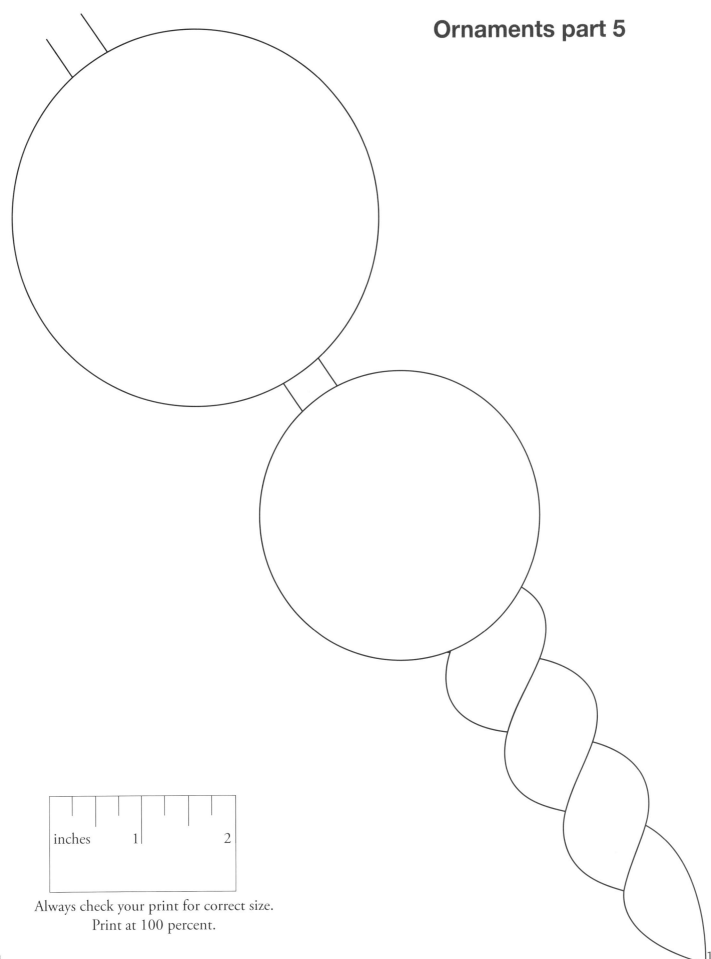

inches 1 2

Always check your print for correct size.
Print at 100 percent.

1

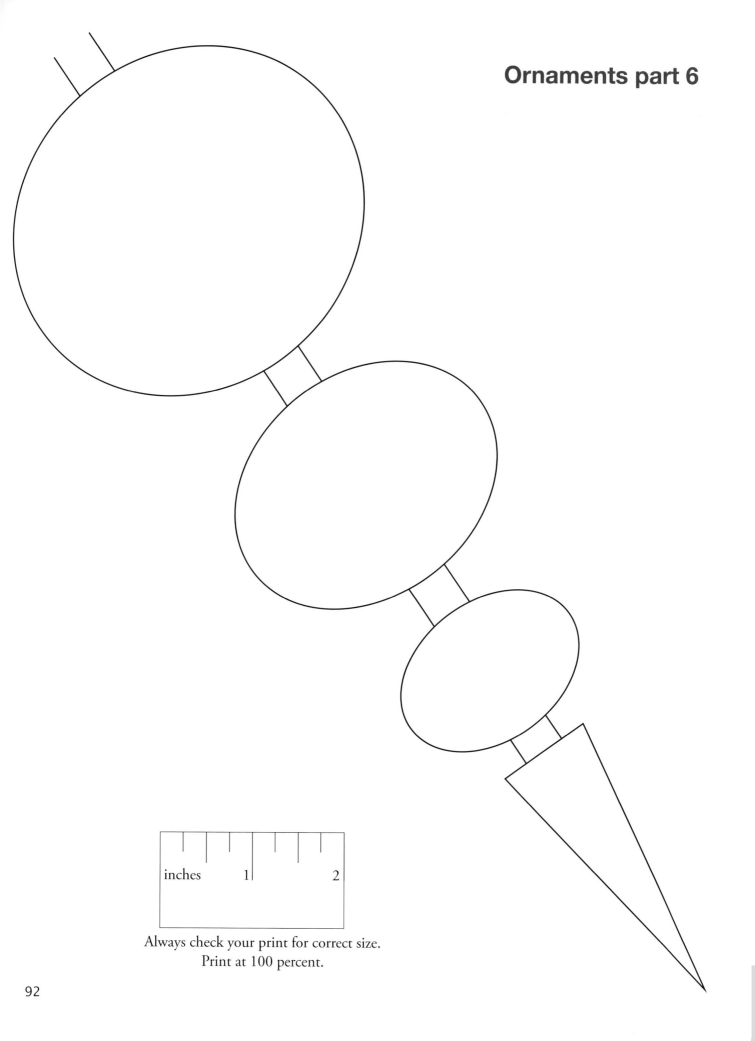

inches   1   2

Always check your print for correct size.
Print at 100 percent.

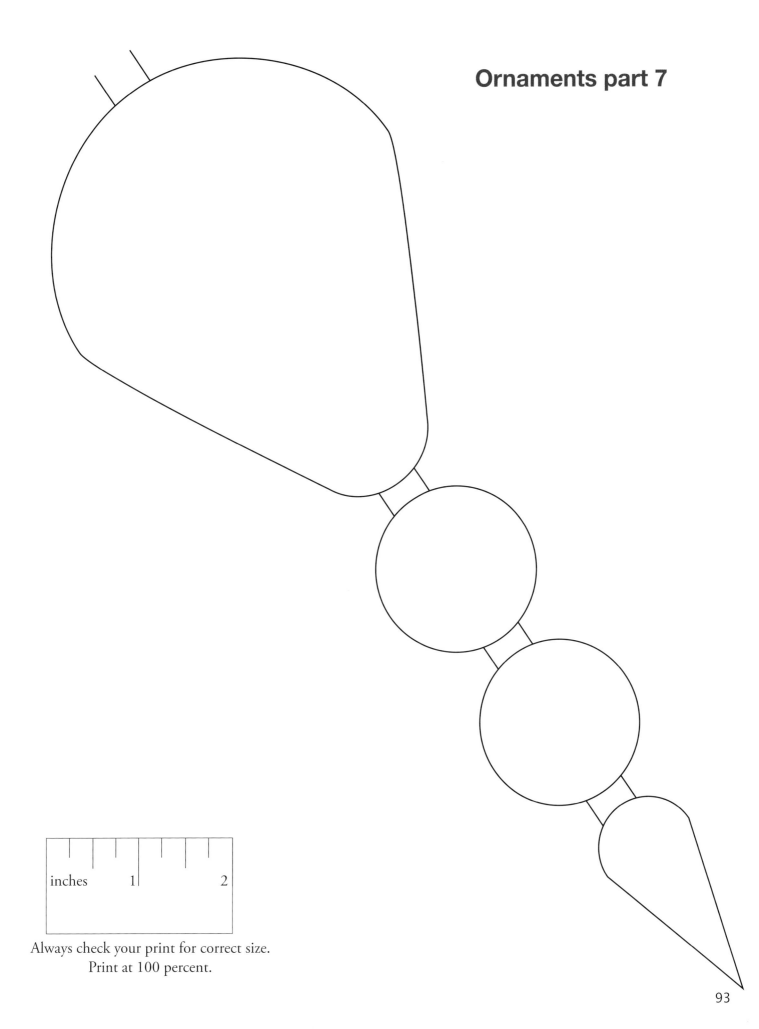

inches   1   2

Always check your print for correct size.
Print at 100 percent.

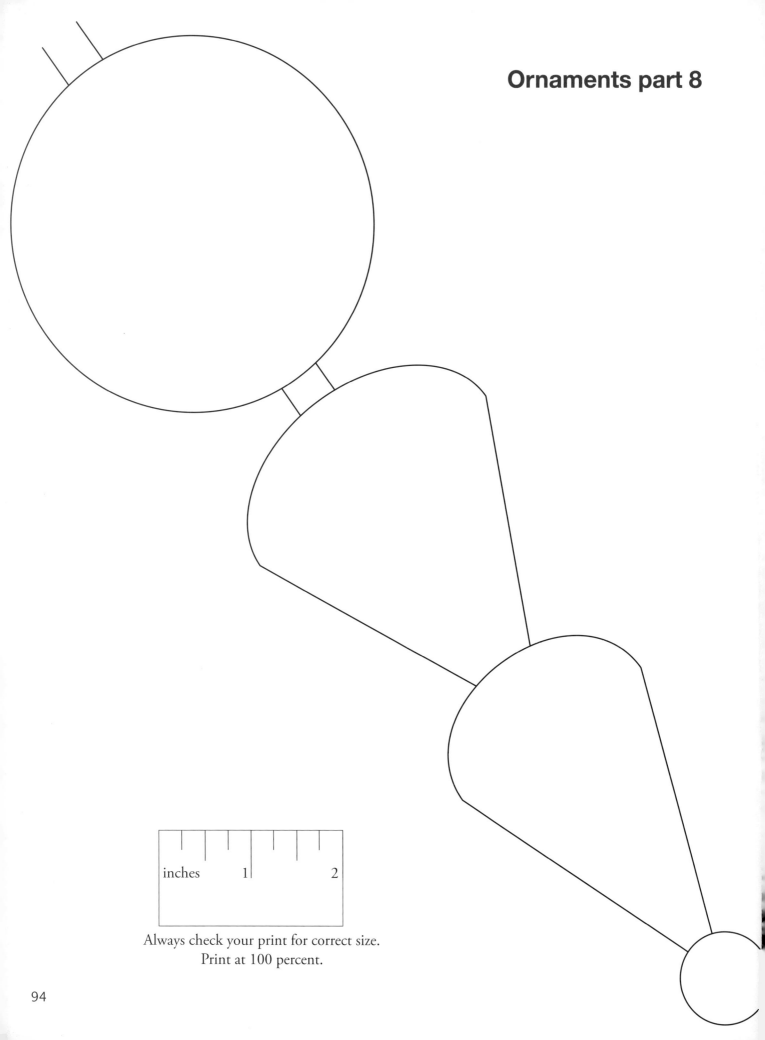

inches   1   2

Always check your print for correct size.
Print at 100 percent.

Jan McGrath, coauthor and a moving force behind this book, unfortunately passed away on February 14, 2015. All of us at Kansas City Star Quilts are thankful we could help make her dream of a Windy City Christmas come true.

Jan was born and grew up in Goodland, Indiana, and was a graduate of Indiana State University. She graciously shared her talent and expertise as the owner and "Queen Bee" of Bits 'N Pieces Quilt Shop in Crown Point and will be deeply missed by her many friends, fans, and acquaintances throughout the quilting world.

Jan's creativity will be carried on by those whom she taught to quilt or helped choose a pattern or select fabrics for a special quilt. Diana will continue to share their dream through Windy City Christmas trunk shows and workshops. We are proud to be a part of her living legacy with the publication of Windy City Christmas. Enjoy and remember.

Marshall Field's south rotunda has a mosaic ceiling designed by Louis Comfort Tiffany. It contains 1.6 million pieces of iridescent glass and took more than four dozen men two years to complete.